MIDNIGHT IN ISTANBUL

A WWII ESPIONAGE THRILLER

KATHRYN GAUCI

First published in 2024 by Ebony Publishing

ISBN: 978-0-6487144-7-7

"One day there occurred a death in the Hoca's village. When the friends of the deceased asked the Hoca where they should take up position while the coffin was carried to the graveyard, he replied: It does not matter where you are as long as you are not in it."

A legendary Nasreddin Hoca story recited by the Turkish Foreign Minister, Hüseyin Numan Menemencioğlu, in early 1944, when asked where Turkey stood in relation to the war.

CONTENTS

CHAPTER 1

ISTANBUL. A PLACE where you can easily lose yourself: an intoxicating mix of the Orient – sweet and sensual – combined with an ever-present sense of adventure, intrigue, and danger. A place where the unknown lurks in every shadow of its famous winding streets and minarets; every nightclub and backstreet cafe; every ferry ride that left you unsure if you would reach the other shore; every taxi ride that made you suspect you were being followed; and perhaps most of all, in the arms of every beautiful woman who declared her love for you. Of all these dangers, maybe it was the last that was the most potent. Why? When a beautiful woman casts her spell on you, even the most cautious amongst us cannot resist temptation. I had long learned that human beings are a combination of strengths and weaknesses, and here in Istanbul, those weaknesses needed to be kept in check, especially if you were a man like myself, a secret agent, posted to the jewel of the Orient to serve the interests of the Allies in a neutral country surrounded by enemies, some of whom were on our side. To all intents and purposes, I was an Englishman, but when I stepped on Turkish soil, something inside me stirred. I was back on home soil. This was the land my Greek parents were born and raised in, a world I had not known existed until much later in my life.

The world was at war, and in a war, one can never let one's guard down, but as I have always been a man attracted to intrigue and danger,

I confess to enjoying a little cat and mouse game every now and again, especially one played with a lover. It relieved the boredom of waiting around, never knowing when an assignment or meeting would take place. After all, a man in my position could not take the future for granted. With this in mind, I decided to savour the delights of Istanbul while I could, much as intrepid travellers had done for centuries before me. I was not the first to be captivated by its charms, and I certainly wouldn't be the last.

I was sitting at a table in one of my usual haunts, the Rose Noir *gazinosu*, an elegant but somewhat shady nightclub just off Taksim Square in Beyoğlu, savouring my third whisky on the rocks and listening to the sultry voice of Ilona singing a Hungarian tango and mesmerizing the audience as she usually did, when one of the hostesses came over to me.

'Mr Caldwell, there's a telephone call for you.' She indicated a glass booth just behind a red velvet curtain.

I had been expecting this call all evening and as it was five minutes to midnight, I had almost given up. I hurriedly wove my way through the packed room, where the patrons were absorbed in drinking and enjoying the club's culinary delights along with the music, and picked up the receiver. 'Caldwell here.'

A man with a deep voice answered. 'Meet me near the Galata Bridge in thirty minutes. On the quay – the the Karaköy side – at the pier, opposite Ali's Fish Tavern. Don't be late.' There was a slight pause. 'Make sure you're not being followed.'

'How will I recognise you?' I asked.

'You won't. I will recognise you.' There was a click and the line went dead.

I went back into the room just as Ilona was taking a bow. The audience clapped in appreciation and from somewhere, a voice called out for more. I called the same hostess over and asked for my bill. As I paid her, I asked her to tell Ilona that I was sorry to leave so early. I would see her later as I did most nights after she finished work. She went straight over to the stage where Ilona, resplendent in a shimmering silver gown, was signing her autograph for an admirer on a glossy black and white photograph of herself and the band – *The Budapest Gypsy Band featuring Ilona Lazlo*. After receiving the message, Ilona looked in my direction and blew me a kiss. She was used to my late-night rendezvous.

Outside, the temperature had plummeted to below freezing. One thing that had attracted me to Istanbul was the thought of warm weather – balmy nights and golden sunsets – but tonight was certainly not one of those nights. It was December, and Istanbul was in the midst of one of its worst winters in years. A strong wind whipped through the city from the north, and to cap it all, it was snowing. The doorman, a stocky fellow clad in a gold-braided uniform, had been there since the club opened some ten years earlier, and like most other employees, had been hired by the club's owner, Boris Andreyev, because he was an immigrant down on his luck. Boris was a White Russian émigré who had arrived in the city at the start of the Bolshevik Revolution. Many of his fellow émigrés had prospered due to his support of Atatürk and his black market connections. Boris had friends in high places and was a man I had been advised by my handlers to nurture due to these connections, even if he was a shady character. For a price, Boris could fix anything.

I slipped the doorman a few liras and he hailed a taxi for me and asked the driver to drop me off near the entrance to the Tünel, a stone's throw away from the Galata Bridge on the Karaköy side. At this time of night, the area would normally have been busy, but the worsening weather kept most people indoors. Only a few desperate vendors were out, shivering in doorways and trying to scratch a living with their trays of cigarettes or carts of hot salep – a drink made from orchid root which did wonders for chest ailments in winter. I pulled up my collar and almost shrank into my overcoat in a bid to keep warm, and made my way towards the pier. By now, my hat and coat were flecked in snowflakes and I hoped my contact would recognise me before I caught pneumonia.

Stamping my feet to keep warm, blowing warm breath on my gloved hands, and cursing him for arranging to meet me in such a miserable place, I stood around looking at the dim lights in the few cafes and taverns that still remained open, wondering about this mysterious man who was so desperate to meet me. It crossed my mind that I might have fallen into a trap, as up to this point, all my contacts had been through Sam Johnson and the Office of Strategic Services, otherwise known as OSS. Earlier that morning, I'd received a strange message given to me by the concierge and owner of my apartment. 'I found this envelope addressed to you inside the letterbox,' he'd said. 'I checked it earlier this morning, so it must have been delivered by hand sometime in the last few hours.'

I thanked him, and in the quiet of my room, opened it with great curiosity. Inside was a note, typed rather than handwritten, as was my name on the envelope. It simply said, *I must speak with you immediately. Be at the Rose Noir this evening, I will call you there. Destroy this letter and don't mention it to anyone. Wait for a telephone call.* It was not signed and the phrase, *don't mention it to anyone,* was underlined. I did exactly as it said. I destroyed the letter. Ilona was out and I didn't say anything when I did see her later at the club.

Now I was wondering what I'd got myself in to. It was at this point that I spotted a small group of people gathering further down the quayside and saw two police cars and a van pull up. With one eye on the lookout for my contact, I walked over to see what was going on. I arrived just as a man's body was being dragged out of the water. It was not the first time I'd seen bodies being dragged out of the Bosphorus – suicides, murders by jealous husbands, or a shady deal gone wrong. I wondered which one it was this time.

I recognized the man in charge, or rather, he recognised me.

'Ah, if it isn't Caldwell Bey,' he called out.

It was Chief Inspector Aksoy: Murat Aksoy, to be exact, of Istanbul's homicide squad. 'What brings you out on a night like this – and at such a late hour?' he asked. 'Looking for a good story?'

After casting another glance over my shoulder to check my contact was not around, I sauntered over. 'I was on my way home from a night with some friends. I had too much to drink and needed to get some air.'

Aksoy knew I was a war correspondent. He also knew I was connected in some way to the British and Americans, but didn't pry too much so long as I was discreet and not a "foreign troublemaker" as he called many foreigners. When the men laid the body on the pier, he asked them to search his pockets.

'What happened?' I asked.

'Someone in the tavern reported hearing two pistol shots. Apparently he happened to be looking out of the window when he saw a man – presumably this unfortunate soul – walk along the pier. It appears that another man was following him. There was a scuffle and two shots were fired. The man fell to the ground and the second man kicked him into the water before running away. Luckily these boats are here as we found him wedged between them.'

I looked over the edge of the pier. Blood smeared the side of one of the boats. The man had been wearing a thick overcoat over a suit. As I watched, a policeman hooked the man's hat out of the water and placed it by his side. There appeared to be nothing in his pockets – not even a wallet.

I took a closer look and it crossed my mind that this might be my contact, but then I wasn't sure what he looked like. I breathed a sigh of relief when I didn't recognise him.

Aksoy, always astute, noticed me taking a good look. 'Whoever shot him made sure there was no identification,' he said. 'He wouldn't be one of your friends, would he?' he added with a grin.

'I've never seen him before. Looks like it might have been a robbery gone wrong.'

Aksoy told the men to take the body to the morgue and do a thorough forensic examination. 'I want to know the results as soon as possible,' he added. They put the body in the police van and drove away. 'Do you want to join me for a glass of raki while I wait for the report?' he asked. 'You look like you could do with something to warm you up.'

As there was still no sign of my contact, I agreed, and we walked across the road to the same dimly lit fish tavern from where the owner had called the police. A few customers sat around the warm brazier.

'A bottle of raki,' Aksoy said to the owner, 'and whatever food you have left on the menu.'

The man brought over a plate of freshly fried sardines, a slice of semi-hard cheese, olives, and a basket of bread. When pressed about what else he saw earlier, he shrugged. 'It was too dark to really see anything. Maybe the man who ran away was middle-aged. I can't be sure. He wore a long overcoat and one of those fur-lined hats with ear flaps.'

Aksoy sighed. 'Just like a few thousand others in the city in winter? Not much to go on, is it?' The man apologised, as if it was his fault.

'At least tonight's death was different to the one last night,' he continued, as he tucked into his sardines with gusto. 'That one was a poor unfortunate prostitute – one of the many nameless victims of her trade. This one looks more complicated, wouldn't you say?'

'I don't know. Do you have many shootings just lately?' I replied, dipping my bread into the olive oil.

'Stabbings are a regular occurrence, but shootings – well, the authorities have a particular dislike of shootings. They are fearful that they may have something to do with the war.'

'Turkey is neutral. Why should a shooting bother them?'

'My dear Caldwell Bey. That is so; we *are* a neutral country, and it is precisely this neutrality that we want to keep. We must be cautious of those foreigners who want to drag us into a diplomatic "issue". Take the case of the bombing in Ankara. That was clearly a case of trying to lure us towards one side rather than the other.' I knew Aksoy was referring to the two Russian secret agents, George Pavlov and Leonid Kornilov, who were locked up in 1942 for trying to kill Ambassador von Papen. 'It took us many years to recover from the Great War and then the war with the Greeks. Our dear president, İsmet Paşa, is an intelligent man – experienced and a clear thinker. He does not want outside powers to bring us undone again. Atatürk, may Allah rest his soul, taught us all that. We want to prosper in peace. Trouble-makers will be dealt with swiftly.'

'You sound as if you think this had something to do with one of us,' I replied. 'Anyway, a foreigner might also use a knife. He might even use his hands and strangle someone. Why put so much emphasis on a gun?'

Aksoy took another sip of raki. 'You are right, of course, and I am not ruling anything out, but Turks are far more adept at using knives than guns. My gut feeling tells me that this has all the hallmarks of a foreigner, Caldwell Bey. A well-dressed man, out on the pier at this time of night in this weather, shot twice – and nothing in his pockets – no identity card. I'd say that was not just a case of robbery. Whoever shot him knew what he was doing.' He wiped his mouth with his serviette. 'You are a correspondent – wouldn't you agree, it looks a little odd?'

I did agree and a part of me was still wondering if he was my contact, who, despite me keeping an eye out, had not turned up. Thankfully, the waiter brought over a plate of halva and Aksoy changed the subject.

'How's that girlfriend of yours?' he asked, referring to Ilona. 'I hear she certainly draws the crowds, which makes Mr Andreyev very happy.'

'Have you heard her sing? I didn't think clubs like that were your sort of thing.'

'I took my wife one evening. It was her birthday and she wanted to go somewhere special. She said her friends all spoke about the beautiful Ilona's wonderful voice.' He gave a thoughtful smile. 'She certainly is something. You are a very lucky man. I must say, Andreyev runs a fine establishment and the entertainment is renowned. He has done well for himself. For someone who arrived penniless from Moscow during the Bolshevik Revolution, he prospered under our great leader while many Russians moved on – France, Italy, Great Britain, or America. Not Andreyev. He says he owes this country his life.'

I had to suppress a smile. Andreyev was one of the shadiest characters in the city, but evidently, he had ingratiated himself with the inspector by giving him a few tins of the finest caviar, and no doubt helped him out with a few "enquiries" every now and again. The fact that Boris spoke several languages, apart from Russian, made him an ideal informer – to the police or to anyone offering to pay a price. He had even slipped a few snippets of information my way, which I either wrote about in my capacity as a correspondent for the newspaper or secretly passed on to my OSS handler, Sam Johnson. I was quick to catch on and played the game accordingly.

Aksoy returned to Ilona. 'How long have you been together?' he asked. 'Must be a while now.'

'A few months. I met her several weeks after I came here, and she's not really my girlfriend. We lead our own separate lives.'

The inspector laughed. 'That's what everyone in Istanbul says. It seems that for a pair who lead separate lives, you spend a lot of time together.'

'Have you been checking up on me?' I asked, more as a joke than anything else.

'Let's just say I make it my business to keep an eye out for my friends. And you, Caldwell Bey, are a friend. I like you and I wouldn't want to see anything happen to you.'

I wasn't sure where all this double talk was leading. 'Why on earth would anything happen to me? I just do my job and mind my own business.'

He laughed, knowing that most foreigners were there for many reasons, mostly to do with the war and under cover of a legitimate business. It was almost two thirty and Aksoy said he'd better get back to the police station as the autopsy report would be in now. 'How about coming with me?' he asked. I was surprised he even bothered to ask me. 'I am a night owl like you.' He paused for a moment. 'That is if you aren't in too much of a hurry to get back to the beautiful Ilona?'

I knew Ilona would not finish at the club until well after three a.m. at the earliest so I agreed.

By the time we arrived at the Sirkeci Emniyet Müdürlüğü – better known as the Security Bureau, responsible for law enforcement of the Republic of Turkey but also affiliated with the Ministry of Interior – it had stopped snowing, but the temperature was still below zero. Even at this late hour, there were still plenty of people in the building busy at their desks writing up reports or supervising late night offenders and victims of robberies and beatings, all of whom I noted were men. No respectable Istanbulite woman would ever think of stepping foot in a place like this until daylight, regardless of whatever crime had taken place. Aksoy's office was on the first floor, a pokey room that reeked of stale cigarettes. Thankfully there was a radiator so at least it was warm.

He asked if I wanted another drink as he always kept a bottle of raki in his bottom drawer. I'd had enough drink for one night and asked for tea. He picked up the telephone and asked someone to bring us a glass. Five minutes later, a young boy, barely a teenager, entered with a brass tray and placed on the desk two tulip-shaped glasses of tea, a bowl of sugar cubes, and two small pieces of baklava. At the same time another man entered carrying a folder.

'Ah, Ibrahim, thank you.' Aksoy introduced us. Ibrahim Kilic was the chief forensic doctor at the morgue opposite Gülhane Park, further up from Sirkeci towards Sultanahmet. 'What do you have for me?' He opened the file, glanced through the photographs and read through the notes. There were a few envelopes in the file too.

'Two gunshot wounds to the torso from the front,' Kilic said. 'No exit wounds, so we have the bullets. That's not what killed him though. He was still alive when he was pushed into the water.' He picked up one of the envelopes and spilled two bullets out onto the desk. '9mm – seems that they are from a Steyr M1912.'

'An Austrian manufacturer,' Aksoy said. 'After Germany annexed Austria in 1938, the Wehrmacht ordered 60,000 M1912 pistols rechambered to 9mm.' He twirled one of the bullets between his thumb and forefinger, taking a good look at it.

'Such a gun would point to the murderer being a German – or Austrian, wouldn't it?' I asked.

'It could be anyone. It's not hard to get one of them – or any type of gun really. Whoever shot him must have known we would find out what sort of gun it was.'

'Not if the man had not been recovered though. If the shots had not been heard, the body would have washed away by now. Who knows where it would have ended up?'

Kilic pointed to the other envelope, and Aksoy pulled out a few scraps of cloth.

'I took the liberty of cutting off any labels from the man's clothing.'

Kilic picked one up. 'As you see, this suit was made by a tailor in Vienna. And I made a note of the shoes. They are from Budapest. Very fine ones, I might add, and judging from the condition, fairly new.'

Aksoy, glancing at the photographs, agreed. When he looked in another, smaller envelope, his eyes widened. 'Well, well! What have we here?' It was a cloakroom ticket from a club in Taksim – the Orient gazinosu. The number was 207. 'This is getting interesting.' He studied the photographs of the corpse carefully and passed them to me. 'Take a good look, Caldwell Bey. Are you sure you haven't seen him before?'

I was just as intrigued as the inspector. Maybe even more, given the circumstances and the reason I was in Istanbul in the first place. I looked carefully. The man was certainly in good shape – mid thirties, dark hair and, by the looks of it, manicured hands. He did not wear a ring and there was no watch – strange for a man who wore fine clothes. I wondered if the killer took it. Kilic pointed to a spot on the man's inner thigh – a birthmark in the shape of a heart. I handed the photos back.

'I've never seen him before,' I replied truthfully. 'And the Orient Club, I don't go there, but I can make a few discreet enquiries if you like?'

'Thank you. That would be very much appreciated. In the meantime, we will make our own enquires, maybe less discreet than yours though.'

He glanced at the clock. 'Now I think it's time you were getting back to the beautiful Ilona. Kilic will drop you off. He is going your way. He's been working long hours and, I am sure, is dying to get home.' I left, promising to get in touch if I found anything out.

Kilic lived somewhere in Nişantaşı, a residential quarter in the Şişli district on the European side of Istanbul, and dropped me off near the Galata Tower. I walked the rest of the way, the streets being far too narrow for his car. When I turned into my street, I knew by the soft light in my apartment on the first floor that Ilona must be home.

There were four apartments in the building. The owner, a Turk from Konya, lived in the larger one on the ground floor, and rented the others out. Of the two on the first floor, I had one and the other was rented by a middle-aged Turkish couple. Above us was an attic bedsit occupied by an old Turk who had lost a leg at Gallipoli in the Great War and who had a hard time getting up and down the rickety, narrow stairs. In fact everything about the building was typical of the area – steep narrow streets with small, cramped houses, some with overhanging windows on the second or third floor. Most of them were in a dilapidated state with dangerous gas and electricity connections that could set alight the whole neighbourhood at any moment. In all likelihood, they were as far removed as you could get from the home I imagined Kilic lived in.

I opened the door thinking Ilona might be up waiting for me. I was wrong. She was in bed asleep, her clothes strewn haphazardly over a nearby chair. I undressed, slipped under the sheets next to her, feeling the warmth of her body, which even in my tiredness aroused me, and kissed the nape of her neck.

She stirred. 'You're late,' she said sleepily.

'You wouldn't believe what happened after I left the club,' I whispered.

'*Édesem drágám!* Sweet darling,' she replied, pulling the sheet further over her. 'It really will have to wait until morning. I've only just got back myself and I am dreadfully tired.'

She was right. I could barely keep my eyes open myself.

CHAPTER 2

IT WAS NINE thirty when I woke up in a cold sweat from a bad dream in which someone was trying to drown me. Ilona was sitting at the dressing table with her back to me, cleansing her face with copious amounts of cold cream.

'Are you alright, *kedvesem*?' she asked, watching me through the mirror. 'You were making strange noises.'

I sat up and reached for my cigarettes. 'A bad dream – likely from what took place last night.'

Ilona finished her cleansing ritual by applying rose water to her face, stood up, and tied the belt securely around her silk kimono. 'You look terrible. Just look at you, you're sweating. I hope you didn't catch a cold from being out in that terrible snowstorm. I'll go and make breakfast and you can tell me all about it.'

She disappeared into the kitchen while I washed and dressed. The aroma of Turkish coffee wafting through the apartment was just what I needed. When I entered the kitchen, she was pulling a basket up through the window which she'd lowered into the street for the simit vendor to put in half a dozen. She reminded me of the women I'd seen in Naples. Baskets hanging from windows everywhere – a practical idea, I thought at the time. As she took them out of the basket and placed them on the table, I noticed her kimono had come loose again, exposing her ample cleavage, and was thankful the vendor had only caught sight of her pretty face.

'Why were you so late?' I asked, as she stirred the coffee in the *cezve*.

'Boris had some important clients – Bulgarians. He said he was concluding a business deal and asked Rozsika and I if we would stay back and help entertain them. He said he would make it worth our while. She indicated an envelope on the sideboard, which looked like it contained a fat wad of money.

Knowing Boris's reputation, his business deal could have been anything from arms, tobacco, and chromium – sought after by all the major powers – to carpets. Whatever it was, he always seemed to have the protection of the secret police, which led me to believe he was playing all sides and doing it rather well.

Ilona brought the cezve to the table and carefully scooped out the *köpük* – foam from the coffee – into the small cups before pouring out the rest. Her blond hair fell loosely over her face and shoulders, partially covering her deep blue eyes. She knew I was looking at her but did not look up.

'And did you – you know – did you have to...?' I asked.

She finished the ritual of the coffee serving and put the cezve back on the stove. 'You mean, did I have to sleep with one of them?' She picked up her cup in the delicate manner of a lady of the Sultan's harem and took a sip. 'Do you really want to know?'

I was conflicted. I did and I didn't. I knew from the first time we met some four months earlier that she was more than a nightclub singer, so it was something I'd had to accept. I thought back to that moment as I sipped my coffee. We were introduced at a garden party thrown by the wife of the British consul, Lady Celia Broadhurst, and I took an instant liking to her. Ilona was a natural blonde with a flawless, almost porcelain-like complexion, and that day, she was wearing a calf-length, sapphire-coloured silk dress with a low décolleté, and a matching pair of bespoke blue sandals stitched with fine embroidery made by a shoemaker in the Grand Bazaar. She wore an extremely long string of pearls which she playfully toyed with when speaking to people, particularly men. It was at this party that I was told by Sam Johnson, who I'd first met in Switzerland, that Ilona was to be one of my contacts. A very important one as it turned out.

Sam could tell I was smitten and advised me to keep our relationship official, not only because of my assignment, but because I would be sorely disappointed as she was not a one-man woman, but against all advice, I asked her out the following week. I knew she had a coterie of admirers but sensed there was a mutual attraction between us. She herself warned me that neither her own work, nor the work that we did together, allowed us to get into a close "relationship". She was a singer with a famous Hungarian gypsy band who travelled frequently throughout Nazi-occupied countries. I'd heard she had quite a few *affaires d'amour* on the side and was normally a cautious man, but Ilona Lazlo was one of the most alluring beauties I had ever met, and I decided I was prepared to put up with her dalliances just to be in her company.

The affaires d'amour, as she called them, were only when it suited her as she wanted to set herself up in a beautiful villa with a pretty garden somewhere back in Hungary when the war was over. 'In war, one does what one can to get by,' she said, matter-of-factly. 'In that, I am no different to thousands of others.' When I asked if she wanted to get married and have a family, she burst out laughing. 'I'm not the marrying kind. I've seen it all before. People fall madly in love, get married, and then one of them decides to have an affair.' She looked at the ring on my finger. 'Like you, for example. I take it there is a Mrs Caldwell?'

I couldn't lie. There certainly was a Mrs Caldwell. Dorothy was living in a comfortable cottage with a lovely garden in the Cotswolds, waiting patiently for me while I helped in the war effort as we called my secret work. Ilona asked if I loved her. 'I think so,' I replied, 'in a sort of settled, comfortable way.' It sounded completely silly and I tried to clarify the statement. Dorothy and I married just before the war and I *did* love her – or at least I thought I did, until Ilona came along. But it was exactly as Ilona said, someone comes along and things change. When I thought about it, I'm sure that was one reason I took up this work as a secret agent. It offered a legitimate excuse to leave home in search of adventure and excitement.

'You see,' Ilona replied with a smile, 'that is exactly what I am talking about.' She reached for my hand. 'Now that we have established our boundaries, Mr Caldwell – or should I call you Elliot – we know where we stand.' If there was one thing about Ilona that stood out, besides her beauty, it was her forthright attitude. 'So tell me, and don't think about it, what are the first words that spring to mind when you think about me?'

'Beauty – excitement – someone I can call an equal...'

'Is that all?' She tilted her head to one side in an alluring manner.

'No.' I was becoming braver by the moment. 'You are the personification of sex appeal, and...'

She raised her eyebrow, playfully. 'Quite poetic, Elliot – and...'

'And dangerous.'

That made her laugh out loud. 'Dear Elliot, édes kedvesem, why on earth should I be dangerous?'

'Because I have fallen for you. I want to be with you, share my bed with you, and that, Miss Lazlo, is dangerous.'

We were drinking at the time and both got carried away in the moment.

'You and I are on the same side in this war. Whatever happens, you can trust me – otherwise we would never have been introduced.'

Ilona had her own apartment near the Pera Palace Hotel, but that night she came back to my place and we made love. A week later, she moved in but she still kept her apartment for appearance's sake. In a matter of weeks, we grew closer. For one thing she called me kedvesem. When I asked what it meant, she said it was Hungarian for 'my darling'. She also pointed out that she only used endearing words with those she cared about, which pleased me immensely. There were things I could never tell her and I knew it was the same for her, but I *had* come to trust her, and as much as we were advised *not* to trust anyone, I felt safe with Ilona. I liked to think she felt that way about me too. I also came to accept her occasional affaires d'amour, unconditionally. It was not what you could call a normal relationship by any stretch of the imagination, but we both thrived on the excitement and I wondered what would happen when the war was over. She would find her dream house in Hungary and I would return to the Cotswolds. It would be as if the war never happened. Or would it?

She watched me sip the köpük from the coffee and then dip my simit in the rest. Istanbul was a food lover's paradise. There was rationing, but it was not as strict as in the war-ravaged countries, and these simple breakfasts were like a feast. 'Have another,' she said, pushing the plate towards me, 'and tell me what happened when you left the club.'

Her words sent a shudder down my spine as I thought about the dead man. 'I received a phone call to meet a man at the pier near the Galata Bridge.'

'Does this have something to do with OSS?' Ilona asked.

I knew I should keep my rendezvous secret, but what had taken place certainly unnerved me and I believed she would understand so I decided to confide in her.

'I don't really know. Sam would have let me know himself if I was to meet a contact, and he would have given me some sort of description too. The truth is, I have no idea who the man was. I received a mysterious note from someone who said he would telephone me at the Rose Noir, which he did, and he arranged a meeting near the Galata Bridge. In such weather, it was beyond me why he should pick such a place, as we could have met discreetly in a cafe.'

Ilona raised an eyebrow, which clearly told me she didn't approve. 'Oh, Elliot, there are protocols, you know.'

'I know, I know. I should have told Sam, but this man stressed not to tell anyone.'

Ilona blew out a thin stream of cigarette smoke and sighed. 'This means that you have been watched by the mystery man. Not good, but do continue.'

'When I got there, there was no one around. He had specifically told me to be on time, and as I said, not to tell anyone, but after what took place, I'm betraying that trust and telling you. Promise me you'll keep it to yourself.'

At first she didn't answer, but I pressed her before continuing.

'Alright, I promise, although I don't like the sound of this at all. If he's been following you, he could have me in his sights too, maybe even Sam. Maybe you are letting Istanbul lull you into its carefree ways and you've let your guard down. You *have* to tell Sam.'

I felt like a child being chastised and chose to ignore her cutting remarks, continuing with the story. 'After waiting a few minutes, I spotted something going on further along the quay. That's when I saw Murat Aksoy with several of his men.' At the mention of Inspector Aksoy, Ilona's eyes widened. For her, his presence meant trouble. 'They had just pulled a dead body out of the water. Apparently the man had been shot and pushed into the Bosphorus.'

'Was it the man you were to meet?'

'I have no idea. I'd never seen him before. The fact that the man I was to meet never showed up made me think it may have been him, but how could I be sure? Aksoy asked me to have a drink with him while the body was being examined at the morgue and afterwards we went back to his office. Knowing Aksoy, I think he was trying to get something out of me. Maybe wondering if the dead man and I were connected and I was hiding something. According to the autopsy, he had been shot twice – the bullets were from a Steyr M1912.'

'An Austrian gun,' Ilona said, matter-of-factly. 'That doesn't sound good.' Ilona might have looked like a beautiful singer – innocent and unconcerned with politics – but in reality, she was an excellent secret agent working for OSS and knew her weapons well. 'Was there an identity card?'

'No. The perpetrator must have taken it. But there *was* something which he'd obviously missed – a cloakroom ticket for the Orient Club.'

'Can you remember the number?'

'207.' I described the man to her and told her about the heart-shaped birthmark on his inner thigh. I could see her mind ticking over.

'I know a few of the girls at this night club. Perhaps one spent the night with him. Let me see what I can find out.' She paused for a moment. 'Maybe those bullets were meant for you, Elliot. Have you considered that?'

I nodded. 'That thought had crossed my mind.'

The Orient Club was run by a middle-aged Romanian, Razvan Antonescu, and like Andreyev, he had nefarious dealings with whoever was prepared to pay a good price. The thing was, it was common knowledge that he was an ardent Nazi. Although he was careful about broadcasting this fact in a neutral country, secrets are not secrets for long in a place like Istanbul, and for that reason, neither the British nor the Americans frequented his club. High-ranking German officials went there, including von Papen, along with a variety of Nazi sympathizers and anti-Soviets from various other countries.

Ilona, as astute as ever, suggested that she go to the club alone as my sudden appearance in a club frequented by Nazi sympathisers would arouse suspicion. 'I have this evening free,' she said. 'I'll go then. In the meantime, I think you should go back to bed and get some sleep.'

That would have been the sensible thing to do, but I knew she was right when she said I had to report what happened to Sam as soon as possible. I finished my breakfast, kissed her goodbye, and said I would see her later.

Ilona caught my arm as I was about to leave. 'Promise me you will be careful, my darling. If those bullets really were meant for you, the next time you might not be so lucky.'

Her words hung in the air like a dark cloud. 'I promise.'

Outside, the severe weather had eased. It was still cold but at least it had stopped snowing. I caught the tram from the Tünel down towards the Bosphorus and then another tram to Sultanahmet. From there I walked up the hill, past the Nuruosmaniye Mosque, known to most Istanbulites as the Mosque of the Sacred Light, towards the nearby Grand Bazaar. Opposite one of the many entrances was an old han, once used as a caravanserai and which was approached by several steps worn into a smooth curve in the centre through centuries of use. Inside was a small courtyard surrounded on all sides by carpet and embroidery warehouses. Near the entrance, another set of equally worn steps led to a higher floor of tiny workrooms used by various craftsmen. One would have expected such a building to be dark, but it was quite the opposite. The courtyard was open to the elements and light streamed inside, collecting in pools of water between two mulberry trees, which, in the bright daylight, shone like mirrors from the melting snow. I headed to the far end of the courtyard. A sign over the door said, *Galeri Pandora: Carpets–Kilims–Tapis.* In the warmer months, mounds of carpets would be strewn outside, tempting a passer-by in search of a fine carpet, but today, all that stood outside the door was a clay bowl of food for stray cats and dogs.

I knocked three times and a young woman opened the door. *'Hoş geldiniz, efendim.* Welcome, sir.' It was Füsun, the eldest daughter of Mustafa, the owner. She always addressed me with "sir" rather than by my name. She beckoned me towards a narrow set of stone steps. 'They are waiting?' she said, her eyes slightly downcast in her shy manner.

Upstairs I found Sam Johnson and Mustafa sitting on a kilim drinking tea. It was evident they knew something was amiss. Mustafa, clad in baggy pants with a red cummerbund in which he often wore his dagger, these days more for peeling fruit or cutting yarn than killing someone, gestured me to join them while Füsun fetched more tea and a tray of sweetmeats accompanied by dried figs, apricots, and a variety of nuts.

'I gather someone was shot last night,' Sam said. 'I also heard you were in the vicinity at the time.'

I hadn't notified Sam about the secret meeting, but there was no point asking him how he knew. It could have been Aksoy himself. He wouldn't tell me anyway, but as my OSS handler, he had spies everywhere and didn't miss much. I decided to come clean and told him the same story I'd told Ilona earlier. I suggested it might be wise not tell anyone else at OSS until the mystery was solved and he agreed. Mustafa agreed too.

There were a few moments of silence while we considered the situation. Mustafa was one of those rare Turks who favoured the Allies rather than remaining neutral, and Sam had managed to recruit him to work for OSS. He was a great help to us, particularly as far as Turkish drivers and couriers were concerned. He was also good friends with quite a few Greeks – an added bonus as we often smuggled money to the Greek resistance. Because of this liaison, he allowed us to meet in his carpet warehouse, away from "foreign-occupied" offices which were monitored by the secret police. All his contacts were trustworthy and extended as far as Damascus since his second wife was from Syria. Mustafa had two wives: Fatma, the mother of Füsun, who lived a comfortable lifestyle in Antalya, and the much younger Aisha, who didn't appear much older than Füsun. Her family was also in the carpet business so it was deemed of mutual benefit for both families to keep on good terms. As Sam once told me, his first wife was quite happy for him to marry Aisha. I found it rather odd – this oriental view of the world – but then who was I to talk.

I told Sam that Ilona had friends at the Orient Club and was going to make a few discreet enquiries. I asked if he had seen anyone from the Istanbul office of Semperit Rubber, the Austrian manufacturer whose Viennese owner was supplying us information about the Austrian resistance. Sam shook his head. 'Let's give it a few days till things cool down – see what else we learn,' he said in his Mid-Atlantic accent – a blend of American and upper British middle-class that reminded me of Cary Grant.

He also told me "they", meaning OSS in Switzerland, wanted Ilona to take some more money to our contacts in Budapest. 'She's scheduled for another tour in ten days' time,' he said. 'The timing is just right.' I felt a lump rise in my throat. The thought of Ilona going back into Nazi-occupied Europe was not a thought I relished. It would be her third trip and I was worried her luck would run out and she would get caught.

Sam saw the flicker in my eye, read my thoughts, and made a tutting sound. 'Elliot. I warned you about getting close to her. She is essential to our network and the risks are high, even though she is a clever woman.'

'The Austrians have asked us for more money for propaganda purposes – printing anti-Nazi leaflets, etcetera. It's urgent as we've just been made aware that the court in Vienna has sentenced another important Communist to fifteen years' imprisonment. We are assuming she was subjected to the Gestapo's usual inhumane treatment, but as yet don't know if they were able to get the names of her fellow Communists here.' Sam was referring to the prominent Communist organizer – Margarethe Schütte-Lihotzky – who had been in Turkey for a while but returned to Vienna in 1940 to help establish a network of Communist

20

resistance groups there on behalf of the executive committee of the Communist Party of Austria, located in Moscow. Shortly after, it appears that she was betrayed by a Gestapo snitch and arrested. No one knew if she would survive, and the Austrian resistance understood just how vulnerable they were – making our help even more vital.

'I have no doubt that they've contacted the Gestapo here in Istanbul, who will be monitoring everyone from the Reich,' Sam said. 'I also heard that some of these Communists frequent the Rose Noir.'

'I wouldn't know. Andreyev is not a Communist. He doesn't want to get involved with all that stuff, especially as he fled the country after the Revolution.'

'True, but maybe he knows who they are. The Germans have been tracking them down since the Anschluss, so who knows what else they might uncover.'

As ideologies went, I didn't have much time for Communism and from what I gathered, neither did OSS, but Stalin was now our Ally and that made the Austrian and German Communists in Turkey even more of a target for the Gestapo. We also needed to be open-minded too because if they were trying to form a resistance network, that could be to our advantage, but as far as the Nazis were concerned, such people were traitors and undesirables. Regrettably, the Soviets weren't interested in them either, thinking they could be Nazi spies, and it was not uncommon for some of these unfortunate people to disappear without a trace. In fact, Communists weren't the only ones that could happen to. We were free in Turkey although many of us working here felt as if we were living on borrowed time.

'They may have new identities,' I added, 'in which case they will not be easy to track down.'

Sam pressed his lips together tightly and sighed. 'Only if they speak a foreign language fluently, which rules most people out.'

My role in Istanbul was to help the Austrian resistance on behalf of OSS. The operation we were working on was to aid what had become known as the CASSIA Network or the Maier-Messner Network after two of the prominent leaders, Heinrich Maier, a Viennese Catholic priest, and

Franz Josef Messner, an Austrian industrialist, and I reminded Sam that my job was not to track down European Communists, to which he replied that anyone could be turned if their lives depended on it, even here. I knew that resisters came with all sorts of ideologies, but being a Communist meant that such people were particularly vulnerable. When I accepted the assignment in the spring of 1943, I was told that Gestapo Headquarters Vienna had already arrested almost 6,000 Communist party supporters.

'The Gestapo would never have been able to obtain such results about Margarethe Schütte-Lihotzky through pure observation alone,' Sam noted, 'which means that someone is betraying the resistance from within.' He didn't want me to forget that, and like him, I was aware that many ordinary Austrians became Gestapo snitches soon after the Anschluss. Whether they were forced into becoming snitches by way of threats on their own lives, or whether they did it because of financial benefits or the need to feel important was hard for us to know, but it *was* a threat to us all working to help the resistance, even here.

'The Turkish government does not want this war to spill over into their territory for fear of causing a diplomatic issue and we have to operate in a "gentlemanly manner",' Sam said. 'See what you can find out about Andreyev's clients.'

I popped a piece of pistachio-studded lokum in my mouth, stretched out my legs, and digested his warnings. Throughout this conversation, Mustafa sat cross-legged on a carpet smoking a narghile, and the sweet smell of Turkish tobacco lingered in the air along with the smell of wool. He offered me a pipe which I gladly accepted. There was something slightly unreal and yet soothing about the three of us sitting calmly on a soft carpet, with our backs leant against cushions and mounds of carpets, smoking away as if nothing in the world mattered.

I very rarely met with OSS agents in official buildings, which suited me fine. Clandestine work was exactly that – clandestine. It was always somewhere where the ordinary public could be seen. We didn't gather together in offices as MI5 and MI6 agents from London did. The Special Operations Executive, more commonly known in the field as SOE, was different. As far as they were concerned, even in London, a meeting was just as likely to take place in a hotel room or a quiet bar as in their headquarters at 64 Baker Street. In fact, SOE, to which I still belonged and for whom I had carried out an assignment in France, was probably the most indiscreet of all, but we got away with it. SOE agents could blend in anywhere. As I inhaled the tobacco, watching the smoke being sucked down from the bowl and then bubble up through the water into the air of the smoke chamber and through the hose, I felt considerably more relaxed than I had the previous night.

'I'm glad you decided to join us,' Sam said. 'Having an Englishman working with us is good. It's a pity your government didn't take the Austrian call for help seriously. They will regret it.'

I was glad myself that I'd made the move to help OSS, but I didn't make that move lightly. I wasn't exactly what you would call your typical Englishman. SOE knew that and so did OSS, which is why they both wanted me. Neither was my name Elliot, it was George. I was in fact, an Asia Minor Greek and was born in Smyrna, now known as İzmir, in what was then the Ottoman Empire. My parents were wise enough to leave before things deteriorated between the Greeks and Turks, and immigrated to England. My real name, and the one on my birth certificate, was Georgios Calligaris and I was two years old when we left. I was named Georgios after my paternal grandfather. My mother died shortly after we landed in London and my father, Andreas, remarried. To win the woman of his heart, Ermine Grainger, whose wealthy parents owned a textile mill in Lancashire, he agreed to their request that we anglicize our names. My father was a true Greek and his heritage meant everything to him, but for love, he went along with it. Henceforth, my father was called Andrew and I was George. Calligaris was changed to Caldwell.

My father had two more children with Ermine – two girls – and I was raised as a typical English boy, with all the privileges a well-to-do family had to offer. Except for the fact that I knew I had a mother who died when I was very young, I was unaware of our past in Asia Minor until I went to Cambridge University. I had an aptitude for languages, and one day, after I accidentally found a photograph of my father and another woman hidden in a book in the drawer of my father's desk, my father sat me down and told me all about my mother and our past. The photograph was of my parents taken on their wedding day in Smyrna. I asked him if he still spoke Greek. 'Of course,' he replied in a whisper,' *and* Turkish. In fact I still dream in Greek, but don't let your stepmother hear that, will you? Whenever I can, I read the occasional Greek newspaper, but I keep that to myself. She would think I was thinking of your mother.'

I saw the tears in my father's eyes and knew he regretted what he'd done, but it was too late now. From that moment on, I resolved to learn Greek and Turkish at Cambridge, along with French and German. My father was delighted, but the secret was uncovered when I graduated with honours. My stepmother wasn't too happy, but at least I could speak Greek with my father when she wasn't around and that pleased us both. With four foreign languages on my resume, I decided to become a foreign newspaper correspondent.

Working as a correspondent, I moved throughout Europe during the few years before war broke out, spending time in Spain during the Spanish Civil War, and then moving between Germany and Austria with a few visits to France. It was around this time that I married Dorothy. I knew a full-blown war was inevitable and I also believed many Germans and Austrians were pro-Nazi. Through my connections with other journalists, I realised there *were* those who opposed Hitler and could see what was happening to the brave ones who spoke out. Naturally, I reported these sympathies to London, but they were reluctant to express their opinions, at least to me. Most of them had not been in the field, mixing with the real people as I had. They sat in their ivory towers, watching on until it was too late.

I had just completed a short assignment in France with SOE, when I was informed about certain people contacting the British in Switzerland, saying they represented the Austrian resistance. They had originally contacted MI6 and SOE, who were dubious and wanted more proof. Since the Anschluss, the Nazis now referred to Austria as Ostmark, and the Nazi officials were known to be some of the most ruthless in the Reich, so it was hard for anti-Nazis to give convincing evidence of an organised resistance to the Allies. SOE called me in one day to say they'd heard that the Americans had been approached by the Austrians in Switzerland, and were giving me the chance to go and work with them as I knew more about the Austrians than most at SOE. There was no love lost between SOE and MI6, and the fact that they were willing to let me go for the time being meant they thought it of extreme importance. At least the Americans were willing to take a chance on the fledgling Austrian resistance, even if we weren't.

The understanding with SOE was that when the time was right and I had made the right connections, I was to inform them and they would drop their agents into Austria to help in sabotage work. At the time, it was thought that security in the Reich was so tight that dropping agents there was not a good idea. However, as SOE did not answer to MI6, they were willing to take a chance, but only when things looked safer.

Maurice Buckmaster and Vera Atkins shook my hand, released me from my French duties, and wished me good luck. They supplied me with a new set of forged documents and enabled me to meet up with Allen Dulles of OSS in Zurich. At that time, I had no idea what my role would be, or even where I would operate from. As I spoke fluent French and German, I half-expected to go to Austria or Germany. There was also a part of me that wanted to go to Greece – the land my father regretted not going to when he had the chance. As Greece was now occupied by the Italians and Germans, I was glad he chose to go to England.

It was in Zurich that I was introduced to the important Austrian rubber manufacturer Franz Josef Messner and his associate, another Austrian called Barbara Issakides, who was a respected concert pianist trained at the Viennese Academy of Music. Messner's company, Semperit Rubber, had branch offices throughout Europe and South America, particularly Brazil. As such, he was allowed to travel freely and, because of his work, had access to the Reich's industrial, economical, and financial secrets. Such a man, if genuinely despising the Reich as we believed, was invaluable to the Allies. Coming from Vienna, both he and Issakides, who I discovered was also from a Greek background, were good friends and often travelled together, she performing at concert halls or to the elite of the Reich, and he for business purposes.

It was in Switzerland that Messner had first contacted the Allies, in a house not far from his hotel in Bern. As far as the Austrians and Germans were concerned, he was a loyal supporter of Hitler, but that did not stop the Abwehr and Gestapo operating outside the Reich from monitoring the couple's movements, just as they did every other person, no matter what their status. Messner and Issakides were risking their lives and we had to take them seriously. Dulles at first referred to the fledging resistance as 05, because this is what they called themselves in Austria. When we learned that one of their main men running the organization in Vienna was a Catholic priest whose name was Heinrich Maier, we started to call them the Maier-Messner Group, and gave them a network name – the CASSIA Network.

We liked Messner immediately. He was a tall, broad-shouldered man with silver hair and he struck us as genuine. Issakides's family dealt in Oriental rugs and owned a successful rug store in Vienna's 1st District. Like Messner, she had an extraordinary presence, especially with her Grecian face and raven hair. It made me think of my mother, who had similar features. After agreeing to see what we could do, it was arranged that we might be better off working from neutral territory, which meant Turkey as Semperit Rubber already had an established office there, as did OSS. Exchanges of information and money could still take place in Switzerland too as Issakides often performed there, but Istanbul was deemed to be easier due to the company already being established there. We were taking a great risk in trusting them, but decided to go for it. Imagine my surprise when I learned that I would be operating from Turkey, the land of my birth. However, it was stressed that I should not let anyone know I was a Greek from Asia Minor, due to their fractured past. Neither did they want me speaking fluent Turkish. It was imperative that I acted like an English gentleman and was to look as though I was learning the language there. But because I understood the language well, I could listen in on conversations and report anything of significance back to my handler.

From the very beginning, Messner gave us information on important military installations in both Germany and Austria, and in return, we supplied money for the resistance, with the assurance that we would drop agents into the field when the time was right. Vital information was gained from the resistance and given to the RAF and American Bomber Command, who were now operating in the UK, and in August 1943, 324 Lancasters, 218 Halifaxes, and 54 Stirlings successfully bombed the Peenemünde Army Research Centre on the Baltic coast of Germany in what was known as Operation Hydra. More raids followed. The Austrian resistance had shown they were genuine and up until this point, everything seemed to be running smoothly.

After an hour or so at Mustafa's, Sam and I left the han, went for a long walk, and then had a glass of raki in a small bar on the outskirts of Fener, where most of the Greeks in Istanbul still lived. The bar was run by a Greek called Ilios and was situated opposite the battered remnants of the old Sea Walls that used to close Constantinople off from the Golden Horn. It was an interesting area with back streets full of two- and three-storied terraced houses, many with *cumbas*, bay windows in the Ottoman style, as well as a handful of much grander houses. The Ayakapı gate leading through the walls was believed to have been designed by the great architect Mimar Sinan in 1562. It was in this area that the Greek Patriarch lived. After the Great War and the War of Independence, few Istanbul Turks ventured here now, their distrust for the Greeks still running deep in the city. The few Turks who did visit the area usually belonged to the Security Bureau.

Most of the wealthier Greeks left after 1923, and the once grand houses converted to house cafes, restaurants, and tourist accommodation. Ilios was an important connection with the Greek resistance operating in Istanbul. Over a few glasses of raki, we chatted with him for a while and gave him an envelope of money to help his men who were aiding the resistance along the Aegean coast. These operators often worked with Turkish villagers and fishermen who chose to aid the Greeks struggling against German and Italian repression despite one time fighting a war with them. These people preferred to remember the years of shared friendships rather than the politics of today, which they couldn't understand at all. Ilios told us that the resistance used our money to buy safe passages for both Orthodox and Jewish Greeks to get them from Antalya to Cyprus. So far it was working out well. 'They are our brothers. We must do what we can,' the villagers said to Ilios. It never ceased to amaze me that after such bitter fighting, they still held respect for one another.

This was in sharp contrast to Ankara and Istanbul, where politics permeated everyone's lives. Seemingly, the Turkish authorities were turning a blind eye to the Greeks along the Aegean so long as they paid baksheesh and moved on quickly. The last thing they wanted was another incident with Greece after the population exchange of 1923. Knowing that at least some of our work was bearing fruit, I then parted ways with Sam, called into Ross's bookshop, one of the few centres for British propaganda in the city, to buy some magazines for Ilona. Most bookstalls and kiosks were hung with German publications, the main one being *Signal* magazine, and during my time here I'd found it almost impossible to discover any single British periodical less than one or two months old.

I made my way across the city just before sunset as the muezzin's mellifluous chants were calling the faithful from the minarets. In front of all the mosques, men were washing their feet at the ablution fountains and the city was extraordinary peaceful.

Back at the apartment, Ilona was waiting for me. 'How did you get on at the Orient Club?' I asked, handing her an edition of the Turkish film magazine *Yildiz* and the latest copy of the German fashion magazine *Modenschau.*

'You'll never guess who I passed on his way out of the club,' she said, quickly flicking through *Modenschau.*

'Let me guess – Inspector Aksoy.' It was hardly a surprise.

Ilona laughed. 'I think he guessed why I was there, but was most courteous, wishing me a good day and telling me that his wife enjoyed my music.'

'Did he say why he was there?'

'Why should he? He would have guessed you'd already told me about the cloakroom ticket.' Ilona sat on the couch with her feet up and lit up a cigarette whilst continuing to admire the fashions. 'It was pretty quiet at that time of the day so I had a drink in the bar with one of the girls, a German friend called Mathilde who told me that Aksoy showed everyone the photo of the dead man which had obviously been taken in the morgue, and mentioned the cloakroom ticket. "It turned our stomachs seeing something like that," she said.'

'Did anyone recognise him?' I asked.

'Unfortunately, Antonescu took charge, saying he couldn't recall seeing him, and naturally, everyone took the lead from their boss, and shook their head. The girls had had it drummed into them that trouble with the police was bad for business. Antonescu said the ticket meant nothing as it didn't even have a date on it. It could have been a few days ago or a few weeks – months even.'

'Hmm, so Aksoy left empty-handed. That's not like him.'

Ilona agreed. 'I doubt he believed them, but what could he do?'

'What about you? Did you manage to uncover anything?'

She crossed her long legs in a sexy manner, and smiled. 'Of course.'

'Tell me. Don't keep me in suspense.'

'Well, I was biding my time with a drink and watching the band prepare for the evening's entertainment, which by the way was excellent – a jazz band from Berlin, happy to be in a place where musical tastes are less restrictive – when Antonescu saw me and came over, asking if I'd like to perform with them.'

'What did you say?'

'That nothing would give me greater pleasure, but unfortunately I was under contract with the Rose Noir and didn't want to upset the band or Mr Andreyev.'

I moved her legs and sat down with her, massaging her calves in the sensuous manner I knew she liked. Ilona was a quick thinker. It was one of the many things I found attractive about her. 'And...'

'He was most charming and said that if ever I changed my mind, I would get star billing. When he left the room, that's when Mathilde opened up. I've known her for quite a long time. We met in a club in Berlin before the war. She wanted to be a singer with a band like me, but despite possessing the looks of a film star, never had the voice and became a hostess instead. She said it paid well and she could always pick and choose her customers, some of whom were big shots in the Nazi Party, even though she is not a Nazi herself. When the war started, she left Berlin, went to Budapest, and then came here. She thought it was safer, but soon realised politics dominated Istanbul too, so kept her opinions to herself. Knowing Antonescu's Nazi affiliations, I could tell she was frightened as she suggested we go to the ladies restroom to talk.

'We were there, behind locked door, for no longer than five minutes. It was then that she told me she *had* recognised the man. "Most of their faces, I try and forget," she said. "I give them what they want and that's it. But it was when the inspector said the man had a heart-shaped birthmark on the inside of thigh that I knew who it was." She gave a nervous laugh. "Fancy remembering that rather than his face."'

I stopped massaging her legs and momentarily held my breath. 'Go on.'

'You have to realise that these girls are taught not to pry,' Ilona said. 'It's dangerous and they could be fired. Fortunately, Mathilde has a natural way with men; they feel safe in her company and sometimes say more than they should.'

Ilona's words were reminding me of us. She had that same disarming charm. I brushed that thought aside.

'She recalled thinking how smart the man was and commented on his clothes as he dressed after making love. He told her he used the same high-class tailor as Huber. When she asked who Huber was, he said Franz – Head of Gestapo in Vienna. He also said Ernst Kaltenbrunner used the same tailor too.'

My heart missed a beat. Now I was sure something was very wrong. 'What about his accent?'

Ilona gave a sigh. 'He had a Viennese accent.'

'So he was an Austrian associated with the Gestapo. You know what this means, don't you?' I said.

'Semperit Rubber. They're watching them – and most likely us too.'

'Did Mathilde say when this liaison took place and who he was with?'

'Apparently it was two days before his body was found and all she remembers is that he was with a group. Some she knows work at the consulate here: friends of von Papen. The others she didn't recognise. The place is always full of Germans and their pro-Nazi sympathisers – Romanians, Czechs, Hungarian, French, even Poles, Ukrainians, and Latvians. Looking for his associates would not be easy.'

'So he wasn't at the club on the night of the murder?'

'It seems not. He paid for a few hours with her and left around three in the morning.'

'I suppose this man doesn't have a name, by any chance?'

'Unless the man tells the hostess, they have been told not ask, so she didn't pursue it. How was she to know he would end up murdered?'

'We have to tell Sam immediately,' I said.

Ilona put down the magazine, pulled my hand towards her lace-edged panties, stubbed out her cigarette, and lay back on the couch with her eyes closed. 'Later, kedvesem, later.'

The combination of recent events and sex exhausted us and we slept for a while under a coverlet as naked as the day we were born. When I woke up, she was putting on her dress.

'Sam told me he has another assignment for you,' I said. 'I think he means Budapest.'

'I know. He sent a courier saying he wanted to meet me at the Pera Palace tonight – a casual drink, apparently, which was his way of telling me it's of vital importance.'

This announcement was unexpected. 'I had hoped we would at least spend tonight together as you're not working.'

'Me too, but duty calls.'

'I don't find it at all amusing. A mysterious man has been found dead and you have another assignment which will take you away from me. I'm worried for you.' I watched her tidy herself up in front of the mirror. 'What you're doing is dangerous. Here in Istanbul, it's safer, but in the Reich, in the lion's den, that's something else.'

'Oh my darling, it's what we signed up for, isn't it?'

'All the same—'

She came over and stopped my words with a kiss on the mouth. 'Nothing can be done about it. I will meet Sam as planned and see you tomorrow.'

'Why tomorrow? Won't you come back here afterwards?'

'No. I will return to my apartment. We must at least try and keep up the impression that we live apart, so don't argue. I will see you tomorrow.' She put on her hat and coat and gave another flirtatious wink. 'Surely you won't miss me for one night.'

'Will you tell him what you've found out? About Mathilde, I mean.'

'Of course.'

I gave her a hug and a kiss on the cheek, purposely avoiding her lips so as not to smear her freshly applied red lipstick. 'Be careful.'

With that she was gone and the apartment felt cold and empty, yet her sweet smell still lingered, reminding me of just how attached I'd become to her.

CHAPTER 3

I **SAT UP** half the night worrying about Ilona's meeting with Sam. It would be her third trip on behalf of the Austrian resistance and each time she took a lot of money that amounted to thousands of dollars. The first time, she'd even taken gold coins but they became too hard to conceal. The cash she could hide amongst her many clothes. Because she was a well-known singer, few customs officials dared search her luggage, but it only took one zealot and that was that.

I went over and over the mystery man in my mind and I still wasn't sure if he was the man who called to meet me or the man who shot him. I tried to think if the man on the telephone had a Viennese accent, but it was hard to tell as he only said a few words and there was music in the background. The following morning, I was sitting in the kitchen eating the last simit, which was quite stale by now but softened nicely when dipped into the coffee, when I heard a soft knock on the door. I looked at my watch. It was nine thirty. Who could it be at this hour? I peered through the keyhole and saw Füsun standing in the hallway. She was wearing a cloak with a hood and her head was partially covered with the silk veil, which she always wore. She was carrying a basket covered with a floral cotton cloth.

'Merhaba, efendim,' she said in her usual shy way when I opened the door. My stepmother asked me to bring you some of her sweets. She lifted the cover a little to show me a mound of crescent-shaped walnut biscuits covered with a dusting of fine white sugar. A single clove was meticulously place in the centre of each one.

'Come in,' I said, taking a quick glance down the hall to see if anyone was watching. Istanbul was a city of discreet voyeurs who watched everything from behind gauzy veils, thick curtains, or ornate doorways with small openings; they could view the world, but the world could not view them.

She put the basket on the table, picked up a plate, and arranged the biscuits artfully in a neat conical mound just as they arranged foodstuff and spices in the Egyptian Bazaar. I asked if she would like tea or coffee.

'Thank you. Apple tea will be fine.'

As I took her cloak, I noticed her glance around the apartment. The door to the bedroom was partially open and she saw the bed was unmade. 'Is this where you bring your women?' she asked in a soft voice.

Her direct question took me aback. She gave me a coy smile. 'You don't have to answer that. I can smell her.'

'Füsun!' There was an awkward pause until she picked up two small plates, placed a biscuit on each, and handed one to me. For the first time, she let her veil slide from her head, undid her black hair, which was looped into a bun, and shook it as if enjoying the freedom of not being covered. I had never seen her without her head partially covered and this action took me by surprise. Her hair was beautiful – thick and glossy from regular applications of oil. I was astonished at how long it was. It reached halfway down her back. She sat at the table watching me while I prepared her apple tea and then proceeded to eat her biscuit with her delicate fingers while I looked on awkwardly.

It was not unusual to see women wearing a veil, particularly one that covered the head rather than the face, when in the company of men other than their family members, but since Atatürk formed the Turkish Republic in 1923, women were freed from wearing it. They were encouraged to get an education and follow Western standards rather than those of the East, which he deemed had held the Ottoman Empire back, particularly in the latter years. In cities like Ankara, İzmir, and Istanbul, such women were becoming modern, emulating cinema stars and singers, aspiring to get university degrees and run their own businesses – whilst, it must be said, retaining their feminine charms.

Füsun was not like these women. Her father was extremely conservative. Even though he respected and admired Atatürk, he straddled two worlds – the old and the new. Mustafa had two wives and his daughter's education was basic. From an early age, much of her learning was all about recognising a good rug from a bad one and how to repair the worn ones. As both of her father's wives were in the carpet business, it was highly likely that she too would marry into the trade.

I always thought of Füsun as a woman in the shadows, someone who was brought up to obey her future husband as she obeyed her father. Sam warned me from the moment I came here not to take up with a Turkish woman. 'Off-bounds,' he said in his matter-of-fact way, but the way she was looking at me in that moment made me wonder if I really understood Turkish women at all. I was struck by her deep brown eyes flecked with gold in the dappled morning light. They were looking directly into my soul and it unnerved me.

'This is the first time I've really seen your eyes,' I said. 'You usually avert them from our gaze.' By our, I meant Sam and I. 'You shouldn't do that, they are beautiful.' She popped the last piece of biscuit in her mouth and wiped her hands.

'It is said that the eyes are the window to the soul,' she replied after a while, her voice deliciously soft and warm. 'Can you see into *my* soul, Caldwell Bey?'

Seeing and talking to her like this was so unexpected that I felt a warm quiver in my groin. I was attracted to her mysteriousness, just as Pierre Loti had been attracted to Aziyadé. Is this how oriental women act, I thought to myself? Saying so little; doing hardly anything, yet setting a man's heart on fire. Is that how it worked?

She smiled. '*Efendi*, your cheeks have reddened. I'm embarrassing you. I apologise.'

'Not at all,' I lied. 'It's just that I didn't expect to see you here.' I offered her more apple tea while I grappled with my senses.

'Actually, there's another reason I'm here.' By now I wasn't sure what to expect. 'I have a message from Johnson Bey. You are to pick up some money from a Greek man called Theo who lives in Fener, one of the old

Greek neighbourhoods. He runs a grocery near the Church of Panagia Mouchliotissa Theotokos Panagiotissa. It's near the Patriarchate.'

'Who is the money for?'

'I believe you are to give it to the concert pianist who will be performing at the waterside mansion of the industrialist Irfan Kulin this evening. The performance will be attended by von Papen.' She paused for a moment. 'By all accounts, the pianist is famous in the Reich.'

I listened carefully. This could only mean Barbara Issakides, but why had Sam not told me this himself? 'Go to see this man during evening prayers. Pick the money up and leave immediately. Don't give it to your Hungarian friend.' I knew she meant Ilona as she glanced away shyly when she said it. As if reading my thoughts, she told me that Sam would be at the concert too, but in the company of someone from the United States embassy and he didn't want us to be seen together.

'He has arranged for you to go with Lady Broadhurst, whose husband is in Egypt at the moment. Accompanying this lady will be your excuse to attend the event. Somehow, you must give the money to this pianist personally. Johnson Bey stressed the word *personally*. He says he has every faith in you.'

'I bet he does,' I replied, rather sarcastically. A few hours earlier, I was worrying about Ilona getting caught; now I was worrying about getting caught in the act of giving money to an Austrian resistant.

She stood up to leave. 'Thank you for coming,' I said and picked up her cloak, holding it open for her to slip it around her. Instead, she put her hand on my chest and moved closer and kissed me on the mouth.

Instinctively, I took a step back. 'Füsun... What are you doing?'

She reached for my hand. 'I always wondered what it would be like to make love,' she said, her voice soft and velvety again. 'Like the women you have here. *I* want to be one of those women.'

I pushed her hand away. 'Stop! You're making a mistake. Firstly, I don't have women here, and secondly, well...to put it mildly, your father would be very upset.

'He wouldn't have to know. I can be *very* discreet.'

I moved away further and she grabbed my arm. 'Be sensible,' I said firmly. 'Go home now, before...'

She clutched onto my arm desperately. 'Is it because I am a virgin? Don't you like virgins?'

I was still grappling with her inexplicable behaviour and didn't want to offend her, yet her forthright and matter-of-fact talk was making me ill at ease.

'Dear Füsun, you are a sweet and genteel woman, and you cannot lose your virginity to a man like me – a foreigner who you know you can never marry.' I had to be hard with her. 'Your father would kill you if he found out what you'd done. You will have dishonoured the family. Then he would kill me for dishonouring a friend. Do you want to see us dead? Please leave before something happens. Don't tempt me. I am not the man for you.'

To my great surprise, she began to sob. 'I have fallen in love with you, Caldwell Bey. It is you who must take my virginity. I want to do it with you. I trust you.'

She was trying to be romantic, yet it turned out to be anything but that. In fact, it was most unnerving and I was getting worked up. She was offering herself to me and I was offending her. 'I already have a wife. I cannot betray her.' I tried reason with her, but she refused to listen.

'No. You have a lover. I know you do. I can smell her.'

She started to unbutton her top, but I quickly stopped her. 'If your future husband discovers you are not a virgin, you realise what will happen, don't you? He will not want you, and he will tell your father.' The thought of a honour killing reared its ugly head again.

She laughed. 'There *are* ways, you know – a small operation – or a little chicken blood. We women have ways that men don't know about.' She smiled, but she was deadly serious. 'I want to experience sex with you. Please.'

I looked at my watch anxiously. 'No!' There was a tinge of anger in my voice. 'For a moment of pleasure, you will spend a lifetime of regret. Go now. I have an appointment and I will be late.'

Her eyes flashed and then looked away while she gathered herself together, looping up her hair and covering her head with the veil again before putting on the cloak. 'May Allah forgive me,' she said. She picked up her basket and left.

I grabbed her arm as she was leaving. 'You don't have to apologise. I care for you but I respect both you and your father. He will never know what took place today. Go in peace.'

'Thank you.' She lowered her eyes in her usual manner and hurried away.

After she left, I slumped against the door to catch my breath, wondering if I had imagined what had just taken place. I needed a stiff drink and poured myself a full glass of raki. I had enough complications in my life without this: a wife, a lover, a murdered man who we suspected was looking into our affairs, and now someone who wanted to lose her virginity with me. I had always expected Istanbul to be filled with danger, but this was becoming too much. Sooner or later I would end up in the morgue like the mysterious man – a questionable death to be solved by Aksoy and Kilic.

*

At the allocated time, I took a taxi to Fener and asked the driver to wait while I made my way to Theo's grocery shop a couple of streets away. The Greeks were out and about even though the weather was still cold and miserable. I liked Fener; it retained some of its rich Greek heritage, but the Greek community now was only a shell of its former self. Even so, they were still a proud group and loved the city immensely, as my father said he had once loved Smyrna. They also loved their fellow Greeks back on the mainland, which was why so many were prepared to risk their necks to support them. Theo and Ilios were two such men.

My meeting with Theo lasted no more than five minutes. He gave me a box of the best lokum in Istanbul, telling me that the money was in a secret compartment underneath. It was beautifully wrapped and tied with a white ribbon. 'You are to give it to the concert pianist, Frau Issakides, personally. She is expecting it. Don't get into a conversation as her minders will be there. She will recognise this special gift by the way I have arranged the ribbon and the small pink rose tucked into the knot.' When I thanked him, he said that he wished he could hear her play himself as he was aware her family were of Greek origin. I wanted to tell him so was I, but refrained.

'Her family are rug importers in Vienna,' Theo said. 'I believe they have bought fine rugs from Mustafa.' He paused for a moment. 'We must help our friends, particularly those under Nazi occupation.'

I walked back to the waiting taxi to find the driver reading *Cumhuriyet*, Turkey's oldest daily newspaper, which I noticed featured a picture of Barbara Issakides on the front page – *International Viennese pianist gives a recital this evening, hosted by industrialist Irfan Kulin at his waterside mansion, a yalı on the shores of the Bosphorus. German Ambassador von Papen to attend.* I gathered that the driver had no idea who she was as he was more interested in an article about another earthquake near his village in Anatolia.

Ilona was not home when I arrived back at the apartment, and somehow, I didn't really expect her to be. It was highly likely that she too was caught up in these last minute arrangements. I sniffed the air. Füsun was right. I *could* smell the scent of a woman here, even without seeing the array of perfume bottles and jars of cream on the dressing table. I put the gift on the bed, careful not to let the rose slip out from under the ribbon, and prepared myself for the much-anticipated event. Escorting Lady Broadhurst required dressing in my finest clothes: a dark, fine woollen suit tailored in Savile Row prior to the outbreak of war, a crisp white shirt and burgundy-red bow-tie, and a pair of shoes so highly polished, I could almost see my reflection in them. I checked myself in the mirror –smoothing my hair back with oil which smelt of a mixture of frankincense and sandalwood, recommended by my barber in Pera–and couldn't help wondering how it was I ended up here. I could have just as easily been stationed in a country where such an evening's entertainment would not have been possible. Lastly, I picked up my camera as I would be there in my capacity as a correspondent for the New York Times and would need a photograph to accompany my article.

The snow and cold and sharp wind had ceased for the moment, and I walked to Lady Broadhurst's home at the consulate near Taksim to collect her. I was early and her butler ushered me into the sitting room, where there was a warm fire. He poured me a cognac while I was waiting. I sat in the armchair and picked up the latest American newspaper, flicking through the pages about the progress of the war. Despite constant German bombing raids in England and the Soviet Union, there was no doubt the Germans were facing defeat, which made what we were doing all the more dangerous. The Abwehr and Gestapo had always kept Hitler and his cronies up to date with what was going on, but these days the presence of so many Gestapo agents and collaborators made things worse. They were notoriously relentless in hunting down their prey.

The clock on the mantelpiece chimed seven and the door opened. Lady Celia was clad in a long sable coat and wore her hair up, with an exquisite aigrette in the shape of a half-moon, studded with tiny diamonds and sapphires, out of which sprouted a wispy, pale blue ostrich feather. She was followed closely by her Pekinese, who she referred to as "Gonca", a Turkish name for a girl meaning rosebud. Little Gonca was a snappy, spoilt dog and anything but a sweet and delicate rosebud. I had twice been bitten by her and quite disliked her. She made a beeline for me but Lady Celia called her back, admonishing her like a child. 'Naughty Gonca. Leave the nice man alone.'

I presented Lady Celia with a bouquet of flowers, a small token of appreciation at being asked to escort her, and at the same time told her the package was the best Turkish lokum for Frau Issakides. She most likely knew it was more than a gift, but was far too discreet to say anything. 'Thank you for agreeing to accompany me tonight, Elliot. I always enjoy your company. I am afraid Dicky will be most disappointed not to have been able to be here. He is an ardent admirer of Frau Issakides.'

Dicky – Sir Richard Broadhurst – was at another conference with the Allies. I asked if there was any progress, and she laughed in response. 'Winston is constantly trying to persuade the Turks to join us, but I am afraid that he is not getting anywhere.' By Winston, she meant Churchill, a man she'd met on many occasions and was on first name

40

terms with. 'Winston lost at Gallipoli and he's still losing, poor chap, at least as far as bending the minds of the Turks is concerned.' She wagged her finger and smiled. 'But he is like a dog with a bone, and sooner or later he will achieve his aim.'

I wasn't so sure. From what I gathered, he had a lot to contend with. Mussolini might have fallen in Italy, but it was of little consequence to the Turks. For them, the Germans were far too strong, as was proven in Greece: they had taken the Dodecanese Islands and were on the Bulgarian border, far too close to Turkey. If Germany got wind of Turkey being in anyway pro-Allies, the Luftwaffe could destroy İzmir and Istanbul easily. Apart from that, the Turks were a wily lot and kept a polite, genteel face when attending these international conferences – and there had certainly been a lot of them: Casablanca, Cairo, Adana, Moscow, Tehran, and now Cairo again. I knew the British. They took the Turks at face value and just didn't understand their nature. Sir Richard, who spoke Turkish, was an exception. He warned them not to push things too far. He also knew President İnönü and Foreign Minister Menemencioğlu personally. At the Adana Conference, headed by İnönü and Churchill, İnönü showed extreme reluctance to join the war. The other members of the Turkish side –Prime Minister Şükrü Saracoğlu and Field Marshal Fevzi Çakmak, along with a retinue of advisers – were equally dubious.

Churchill's lavish promises of military help, code-named Operation Hardihood, and the list of military equipment drawn up, known as the Adana Lists, which Churchill said would provide Turkey with war material "to the full capacity of Turkish railways", was also met with scepticism. In turn, Churchill requested access to Turkish air bases for the RAF so that the British could bomb the oil fields of Ploieşti in Romania, the principal source of oil for Germany and their positions in the Dodecanese. Churchill made it quite clear that if Turkey refused to join the Allies, he would not try to stop the Soviets from moving to control the Dardanelles. Needless to say, the Turks were still not persuaded.

'I think Churchill has a lot on his plate with the Americans and Soviets,' I said. 'Satisfying everyone is impossible.'

Lady Celia shrugged. 'Dicky is worried that von Papen seems to be aware of everything that is going on from our side. He suspects a spy in our midst, especially when von Papen started to talk of concentrations of German troops in Bulgaria one evening.' She realised she had said more than she should and clarified the situation. 'I am telling you this in confidence due to our close friendship and so you might try and use your contacts to find something out.' She pulled on her kid gloves and said it was time to leave. 'Let's not sully our evening with politics. We will enjoy ourselves with a night of Chopin. Come on, the car's waiting.'

It was the first time I'd been to Irfan Kulin's mansion. Located in the Beşiktaş district, it was, as I expected from someone of his wealth and stature, impressive. Diplomatic number plates automatically allowed us to pass through the tall gold and black gates, designed after the style of those at the nearby Dolmabahçe Palace. The chauffeur drove us to the entrance and then parked the car to wait. The light in the portico was ablaze from ten crystal lanterns hanging in a central row from the ceiling, each of them surrounded by gold arabesques. As we entered the hallway, someone took Lady Celia's coat, revealing an elegant midnight blue satin dress with an embroidered bodice in silver and turquoise, which set off her aigrette beautifully. She was in her late forties yet still possessed the figure and complexion of a much younger woman, the result of holidays hiking or skiing in Switzerland and swimming in the Mediterranean before the outbreak of war.

A waiter approached with a tray laden with glasses of champagne – Dom Pérignon – a delightful change from the raki I was becoming accustomed to. There were also glasses of blood-red orange and pomegranate juice for the non-drinkers. Lady Celia looped her arm through mine and we entered the salon where the entertainment was to take place. Immediately, I noticed the large Turkish flag, which acted as a backdrop near the grand piano where Frau Issakides was to perform. At least, here there were no swastikas or Union Jacks, nor the star-spangled American flag either. This was neutral territory, and Kulin was a staunch Turk whose father had fought with İnönü and Mustafa

Kemal against the Greeks. For his loyalty, the family had been rewarded with contracts to rebuild a broken empire. Since the father passed away, Kulin, the only boy in the family, had inherited everything. He became a millionaire overnight, supplying whatever was needed to foreign customers, regardless of which side of the war they were on.

He was a handsome man in his late thirties with a smooth complexion and a neat moustache. Extremely cultured, he spoke several languages fluently – a most convivial and genteel man. His wife, Banu, was quite beautiful and equally as charming. She was an artist who had studied in Paris, and as such, her paintings decorated the mansion alongside other well-known artists, both European and Turkish. Occasionally, she and Lady Celia spent afternoons together playing bridge or tennis, taking tea, or going to art auctions, of which there seemed to be quite a lot despite a war going on.

A quick look around the room told me there were probably about a hundred guests, many of them from the various embassies and consulates, as well as other men of importance, including members of the government who were not attending the conference with the Allies, and other industrialists and company officials. My eyes settled on von Papen, who was engrossed in a conversation with Kulin and several other Germans. To my great surprise, I noticed Herr Messner was with them too. It had been a surprise when I heard Frau Issakides was in Istanbul, but Messner – well, why had Sam not mentioned he was here too? When I met him in Switzerland, I was aware that he and Issakides often travelled together and there were rumours of an affair, but Sam had assured me that was not so. It just suited them to be together for their resistance work. 'Keeping an eye out for each other,' Sam said.

As soon as Banu saw Lady Celia, she made her way over, her rose-coloured silk *robe du soir* by Mainbocher swishing around her petite feet as she walked. She said she was sorry Sir Richard was "otherwise engaged" as she tactfully put it and wanted to know what I was doing in Istanbul. I told her I was a correspondent for the New York Times and asked if I could report on the event, which was why I had my camera with me. Lady Celia added that I wanted to present Frau Issakides with small gift to remind her of Istanbul.

'Let me guess,' Banu said with a smile. 'Lokum. All our foreign guests love it.'

To stop Banu asking any more questions about my work, Lady Celia also added that I was a writer working on a novel.

'Really!' Banu raised her eyebrows. 'May I ask what it's about? Not the war, I hope.'

'Not at all. It's a crime novel set during the last century.'

She looked quite relieved. 'Well, Mr Caldwell, I am sure you must have found out there were lots of intrigues going on at that time.' Just as today, I thought to myself, except that these days they were not set in the Sultan's palace. 'When do you expect to have it published?' she asked. 'I would dearly like to read it.'

'I'm afraid I'm only halfway through.'

Banu laughed. She had a beautiful, playful coquettish smile and my mind flashed back to Füsun. 'Well, don't forget to give me a copy. I shall look forward to it.' I assured her she would have a personally signed copy.

At that moment, someone came over and whispered in her ear.

'It's time for the evening's entertainment. Let me accompany you to your seats.' She ushered us towards the front, her slender arm jangling with an assortment of expensive diamond bracelets.

We were seated in the second row with a couple of other English and Americans. As I put my gift under my seat, I noticed Sam Johnson at the very end of the row. He was with his American friends from the consulate and a glamorous redhead who appeared to be his companion for the evening. He glanced in my direction and discreetly showed no sign of recognition, but he did give a nod to Lady Celia. There was no sign of Ilona, but I hadn't really expected her to be here. This was hardly the place for a cabaret singer. I'd never seen the redhead before and wondered who she was. Lady Celia, who knew Sam quite well and was never one to miss anything, noticed my surprise at seeing him with this woman.

'She's an American,' she leaned closer and whispered in my ear. 'A "secretary"'. She gave a little knowing smile and winked.

My focus now was on the Germans and Austrians who had the privilege of the first row seats. Von Papen was an arm's length away from me. He nodded graciously to Lady Celia as he sat down. 'Good evening, Lady Broadhurst.'

'Good evening, Herr von Papen,' Lady Celia replied.

Seated next to von Papen was Messner himself. Our eyes locked momentarily, and like Sam, we showed no recognition of each other. When everyone had taken their seats, the light dimmed and Kulin approached the stage to welcome us to tonight's entertainment. He spoke in adulatory terms about Barbara Issakides's accomplishments and said he was honoured to have her in his home. He thanked von Papen for his part in bringing her to Istanbul. We all clapped as Kulin left the stage. The lighting dimmed, focusing on a red curtain at the side of the stage. One could sense the swell of anticipation in the guests. After a few minutes, the curtain drew back and Kulin walked on the stage again, this time accompanying Frau Issakides. She wore a copper-coloured dress with a long sequined train. The entire outfit sparkled like gold under the spotlight. A fine Art Nouveau hairpiece studded with precious jewels adorned the left side of her dark hair. Kulin walked her to the grand piano while everyone clapped, then bowed and left the stage. In a grand gesture, Issakides swept the train of her dress to one side and settled herself comfortably on the stool. The room went silent while she took a moment to collect herself.

Even I, who had met Frau Issakides in Switzerland, had never heard her play before and was excited despite my nerves at what I was to do later. When she began to play – Waltz in C-sharp minor, Op. 64 No. 2 – I felt goosebumps run down my spine, it was so beautiful. Both my parents played the piano, and I grew up listening to this music. My stepmother, Ermine, used to say that Chopin had a unique way of conveying complex, deep feelings through the piano, and this was certainly the case now.

As the gentle music of Chopin drifted through the room, I had a clear view through the French windows of the undulating watery reflections of a glorious full moon on the Bosphorus with the soft lights of the fishing boats bobbing up and down, and in that moment, I almost forget about the mysterious phone call and the murdered man. But the presence of Nazis in the room and the fact that, like myself, Frau Issakides was here on a very important mission against such people, brought me back down to earth.

After a half an hour of some of the most beautiful music I'd ever heard, Frau Issakides stood up and took a bow. Everyone stood and showed their appreciation with more enthusiastic clapping. Von Papen walked on stage, presented her with a large bouquet of flowers, and kissed her hand. He made a speech in German about how delighted they were to have her perform in Istanbul and that it would be an evening they would never forget. Kulin made another short speech and then told everyone they were to enjoy the rest of the evening with more drinks, canapés, and dancing.

Knowing I was writing an article on the event and had a gift, Banu approached and asked us to follow her. 'Come along,' she said. 'Better to meet her now because later, she will be entertained by the Germans and there will be no time.' Tactfully, Lady Celia told me to go alone as she wanted to catch up with friends.

We walked a short distance down the hallway behind the stage to a room where two men speaking German were standing guard outside. One, I recognised by his uniform, was German, and the other was a Turk, assigned by Kulin himself to take care of Frau Issakides. Banu knocked on the door.

A voice called out in German. *'Herein.'*

I followed Banu into a room filled with bouquets from appreciative admirers. With Issakides was Messner himself, von Papen, and two men from the German embassy who immediately noticed my camera. A middle-aged woman with greying hair swept back in a bun, who I gathered was Issakides's maid and aide, was laying out an evening dress for her to change into. In German, Banu excused herself for interrupting and introduced me, saying that I was a journalist from the international press and wanted to write about this evening's event. Would it be possible to have a photograph to accompany the article? Barbara Issakides said she would be only too honoured. I steadied my camera and took a shot of her holding a bouquet of flowers. Then, I asked von Papen if I could take a shot of the two of them together. Until that moment I could tell he viewed me with suspicion, but the fact that he would also be featured in such a prestigious newspaper as the New York Times delighted him. It was useful propaganda. I also asked Herr Messner if he would like to have his photograph taken with them as well, to which he happily agreed.

The photographs taken, I gave her my present. She took one look at it, fingered the bow, and threw Messner what I considered to be a knowing glance. Banu said it was something to remind her of Istanbul and a great favourite of all Turks.

'I do hope it's what I think it is.' She gave me a warm smile. 'For once, I shall throw away my diet and enjoy these delicious sweets. Thank you, Herr...'

'Caldwell,' I said shaking her hand. 'The honour is mine. Your talent is exceptional and I shall remember this occasion with great fondness.'

There was a small pile of presents on the table, but Issakides gave the present to her maid and asked her to keep it somewhere safe. 'Goodbye, Mr Caldwell. It's been a pleasure meeting you.'

My mission accomplished, right under the nose of the German ambassador *and* Messner, I left the room with Banu to mingle with the rest of the guests. It had come as a shock to be under the same roof as the Nazi ambassador and the two major Austrian resistance players, and my heart was still beating rapidly. From across the buffet table, I saw Sam watching me closely. He looked pleased to see that I had given her the package as planned. I took a small gold-edged plate and placed a few delicacies on it, including Beluga caviar, and walked over to the French window to admire the view. A small band started to play a fox trot and people began to dance, spilling out on to the terrace, which was completely enclosed by glass windows and heated to keep out the cold. I could only imagine how spectacular it would be in the summer when the windows were thrown open and the fragrance of jasmine and gardenias mixed with the salty sea air. Kulin had certainly done well for himself.

A Turkish journalist acquaintance approached. 'Are you writing an article too, Caldwell Bey?' he asked, seeing my camera. 'It certainly makes a change to write about such a wonderful evening rather than the usual theft or murder, don't you think?'

At the mention of the word murder, I wondered how much he knew about the other evening. No doubt Aksoy had given him something to write about, but knowing Aksoy as I did, it would be his version so as not to alarm the officials.

'I don't usually report on such things,' I replied. 'It's usually about how the Turks view the war.'

'I see, and how do you think we Turks feel at the moment?'

His question was pointed and I answered diplomatically. 'It may not be wise to talk about the war when we are guests of Kulin Bey and Herr von Papen. Let us enjoy the evening and leave the war until tomorrow.'

He smiled and shook his head from side to side. 'A true English gentleman. You are right, of course.'

After that remark, we spent the next five minutes discussing Frau Issakides's accomplishments and music in general. There were always recitals of some sort or another in Ankara and Istanbul, and he was familiar with classical music, which made our conversation all the more enjoyable. As the band changed tempo from a foxtrot to a tango, I felt a tap on my shoulder. To my great surprise, it was Sam's escort for the evening, the beautiful redhead.

'Would you care to dance, Mr Caldwell?'

'Please excuse me?' I said to the journalist.

'Not at all.' He gave me a sly smile and I read his thoughts. What a lucky man I was to have such a beautiful woman asking me to dance.

'I'm not really a good dancer,' I said as we adroitly wove our way between the couples to a place near the band. She didn't answer. To the beat of the rhythm, I did my best, taking her in my arms and then letting her guide me – back and forth with her leg entwined around mine one minute and then stretched out in a graceful move in the next.

She wore a chocolate-coloured dress with a high split on the left side, perfect for showing her shapely leg during a tango. I caught a whiff of her scent –oriental and spicy, sensual and alluring. I was just starting to enjoy myself when she put her cheek close to mine and whispered in my ear. 'I have a message from Sam. You must leave now. Go straight home.'

Her words caught me by surprise, and I momentarily missed a step, stepping on her foot. 'I'm so sorry. I didn't mean...' She put her finger to my lips. 'Now.'

'What about Lady Celia? I'm her escort.'

'It's all taken care of. Her chauffeur will return to take her home.'

The music finished and she gave me a peck on the cheek and whispered, 'And by the way, you *are* a good dancer.'

With that she returned to Sam and they moved on to the dance floor. He completely ignored me. It was as if I didn't exist. I glanced around the room, slightly embarrassed. Everyone was deep in conversation, partaking in more delicacies from the buffet table, or waiting for the next dance to start. Lady Celia was on the terrace, engrossed in a conversation with an Englishman who I didn't recognise and two men in Arab dress, and Banu was entertaining von Papen, Messner, Frau Issakides, and the Germans. I caught sight of Kulin near the door and went over to thank him for inviting me.

'I hope you enjoyed yourself, Caldwell Bey. I look forward to reading your article in the newspaper.' As I left the room, he called after me. 'And good luck with the book. Banu and I are eager to read it.'

Outside, I stood in the portico, hoping Lady Celia's chauffeur would recognise me and drive over. Nearby I noticed Inspector Aksoy leaning against a marble column, smoking a cigarette with one of his men. 'Surely you're not expecting trouble on such a glorious evening,' I said, half-joking.

'With so many enemies under one roof, one can never be sure, don't you agree?'

'You are quite right. How are you getting along with the murder investigation?' I asked. 'Any closer to solving it?'

He gave me one of his devious smiles but didn't answer my question. Fortunately the chauffeur had spotted me and brought the car around.

'Are you leaving already?' the chauffeur asked. 'I was told it would finish around midnight.'

'I need to get this article written to send away as soon as possible. Could you drop me off in Galata? I can walk home from there. It will give you lots of time to get back.'

I bid the inspector a good night and wished him the best of luck with the investigation. The car swung out of the gates and we drove along the seafront for a short while before turning up the hill. The inclement weather had eased, and across the water, dotted with the twinkling lights of fishing boats, the dark shadows of the mosques with their large domes and pencil-thin minarets glinted in the moonlight, like the backdrop of a *Karagöz* shadow puppet play. It was just the sort of sight I'd imagined when I decided to take on this mission, and just as mysterious as it had been since its very beginning all those centuries ago. I only hoped I would outlive this war to experience more of Istanbul's splendour.

CHAPTER 4

I BREATHED A sigh of relief to find Ilona back at the apartment. She was lying on the bed in her flimsy nightdress, displaying her feminine curves like a fine Phidias sculpture in the soft lamplight. I took off my coat, poured two whiskies, and handed one to her.

'You're back early,' I said, sitting next to her on the bed and taking off my shoes. 'No late night?'

'Not many patrons this evening, so we finished earlier. How did your evening go? How was Frau Issakides?'

I took one of her legs and caressed her foot with its painted cherry-red toenails. She squirmed with delight. 'So you knew where I was then?'

'Of course. Sam told me about the event and advised me to stay away as von Papen's minders would be on the lookout for anyone suspicious. Not that I arouse suspicion, but in such company, I would be considered a chorus girl.' She laughed.

'I took a few photos and will send the article first thing in the morning. I must say, she plays Chopin magnificently. We were all entranced.'

'Did you give her the gift?'

'So you know about that too? Is there anything you don't know?'

'What you gave her is certainly helpful and I will take more on my trip – much more. What they really need though are agents in the field, but it seems that it's deemed too difficult at the moment. Sam hopes the first agents will be in Austria by the time I reach Budapest. He wants them there before the Soviets.'

'That's hardly surprising,' I replied. 'Now that the tide is turning, it's going to be a race between the British, Americans, and Soviets for a land grab. They are all positioning themselves. Were you aware that Messner's here in Istanbul too? He was there with von Papen. Naturally both he and Frau Issakides pretended not to know me. Even Sam.' I paused, remembering the redhead. 'He was with a beautiful redhead. I've never seen her before.'

'Ah, that would be Claudine. She's the American ambassador's secretary in Ankara. I gather she's here for a few days. Sam has a soft spot for her. Apparently she's married and her husband is a pilot serving somewhere in the Pacific, so he keeps it quiet.' Ilona smiled. 'Well, as quiet as one can when you are besotted with someone. His eyes light up, he has a spring in his step, and he's not as stuffy when she's around, which is usually when the ambassador is here. I'm sure you've noticed that he occasionally goes to Ankara for the weekend.'

'I had but I always thought it was for business.'

'Business and pleasure I would say, dearest Elliot. In that sense, they are like us, so who are we to judge?'

'I'm not judging. Good luck to them.'

She moved her leg away. 'I have something for you.' She picked up an envelope addressed to me from the bedside table. 'It was pushed under the door.'

My heart skipped a beat. This time my name was handwritten. 'Is it our mystery man again?' Ilona asked, cuddling closer.

I quickly opened it. Inside was a sheet of paper with nothing on it 'It's the same stationery,' I said. I checked the contents of the envelope, but there was nothing else with it.

'Invisible ink,' Ilona said, with a hint of superiority. 'After what happened the other night, whoever it is from is not taking any chances.'

'Clever girl.' That thought had crossed my mind too. I'd used invisible ink on many occasions and there were several ways to read the message, but the easiest was to hold it close to something warm. I removed the lampshade and held the paper against the hot bulb. 'Let's hope you're right.'

Within a few minutes, a faint message appeared. *Meet me tomorrow at midnight in Fatih. Outside Ismail's cafe on the corner of Hasircilar Caddesi and Tahmis Sokak. Come alone.* I looked at Ilona. She shrugged. 'The Street of the Basket Weavers. That's what the street name means in Turkish. It's between the Egyptian Spice Bazaar and the Rüstem Pasha Mosque. I've been practicing my Turkish. You never know when it will come in useful – like now.'

'I know what it means but I wonder why Hasircilar Caddesi?'

'Maybe because the area surrounding it is a like a rabbit warren. It's easy to get lost around there.'

Any thoughts I might have had about intimacy that night with Ilona were dashed. I reached for the whisky bottle but she stopped me. 'No, Elliot. Get some sleep, kedvesem. You need to keep your mind sharp.'

'Somebody wants me dead,' I said. 'They just got the wrong man last time. Worst of all, whoever it is knows where I live.'

'If they – he – wanted to kill you, they would have done it by now.'

'It could have been a "she". Someone as smart as you.'

She gave a sigh of exasperation and turned out the light. 'Get some sleep, my darling.'

Despite my tiredness, I could not sleep and lay in bed, my senses heightened. A screeching cat sounded like someone being murdered; rats scurrying somewhere in the building sounded menacing. I was on edge and that wasn't good. On top of that, I worried whether all had gone well with my delivery to Frau Issakides.

In the morning I was woken by Ilona shaking me. 'Come on. It's nine thirty.' I jumped out of bed and hastily dressed.

'I've been thinking,' she said, her arms crossed as she leaned against the open door, 'if you go tonight, which I know you will, I would like to tail you, just to make sure you're safe.'

'No! Absolutely not! Besides, you have work at the club. And I doubt Sam would agree. I'm going to see him now.' With that, I grabbed my hat and coat and left the building for the Associated Press office to send my report on the previous evening's event to the New York Times, and then headed straight for Galeri Pandora.

Despite the cold, the streets were packed with people going about their daily business. I entered the han and rang the bell. Aisha answered. 'Merhaba, Caldwell Bey. Come inside and warm yourself by the brazier. I will get you something to eat.'

Mustafa was repairing a rug and gestured for me to sit next to him. 'Johnson Bey will be here shortly. I gather he had a long night.'

I wasn't sure whether he meant talking with other dignitaries or the redhead, and Mustafa's straight face gave nothing away. Aisha must have thought I looked under the weather as she brought me a larger than usual tray laden with cheese, bread, and mulberry jam, besides the usual sweets. She sat down on a cushion opposite and silently watched me eat. I was ravenous and ate everything, making her smile. At the same time, I couldn't help but notice that Füsun was nowhere to be seen, which was unusual.

'I gather you received the message yesterday and made your delivery,' Mustafa said. 'From all accounts the Austrian pianist is quite a celebrity.'

'She certainly is. I don't think I've ever heard anyone play Chopin like that before.'

'That's not what I meant. She's always in the company of many important Nazis and Nazi sympathisers. They are watching her carefully.'

'You mean the Abwehr? The Gestapo?'

'All of them, Caldwell Bey. The Bulgarians, Czechs, Romanians, and the Hungarian fascists too I imagine.' He got up and excused himself to get some more wool from a storeroom filled with bales of coloured yarn. I knew he was right. Even Inspector Aksoy would be aware of that.

'Where's Füsun?' I asked, after a few minutes of awkward silence. 'I hope she is not ill. This weather is affecting everyone.'

'She's no longer with us,' Aisha replied, matter-of-factly.

I felt my throat tighten. What did that mean? She made it sound as if she'd died. A chill ran down my spine. 'Is she alright?'

Aisha adjusted her veil slightly. 'She's fine. She's gone to live in Antalya.'

'Why? She never said anything when she gave me the message.'

'Her father thought it was time.'

'Time for what?' I was stunned. It was all so sudden.

'For her to get married.' Again I felt my throat constrict. Had she said anything about our little encounter? Surely not.

Aisha smiled. 'A father knows when it's time for his daughter to get married. He can sense it – like a flower ready to bloom.'

'I see,' I replied, not seeing at all. I could not imagine my own father being so perceptive when it came to my stepsisters.

'We talked about it and decided to send her back to her mother. There is a very nice man in Antalya who has asked for her hand in marriage. Mustafa likes him and has agreed.'

'I suppose he is also in the rug business,' I said, half joking.

'His family export carpets overseas.'

'In that case, she will be a great help to him.' I realised I sounded a little sarcastic.

'*Inshallah*, God willing. Would you like to see a picture of him?'

Before I could answer, she took a photograph from her pocket and handed it to me. I scrutinized it and felt quite sick. He was at least fifteen years older, quite small, and with a large belly. Füsun was a petite, attractive young woman and I felt deeply sorry for her. Losing her virginity to a man like this didn't bear thinking about. She must have known what was to take place, which is why she wanted me to make love to her. I handed back the photograph, trying to look happy for them.

'I hope she will be very happy.'

'Inshallah, she will give Mustafa many grandchildren. That will make him very happy.'

Mustafa returned with two balls of red wool hand-dyed from madder and started work on the carpet again. As he threaded one end of yarn through a large blunt-ended needle, there was a knock on the door and Aisha went to answer it. It was Sam and he looked as if he'd hardly slept a wink.

'I spent a couple of hours at the mansion after you left. Unfortunately, at no time was I able to get anywhere near Frau Issakides – or Messner.

They were accompanied by Germans the whole time. Messner will be at his office today and I've sent a courier to say all is fine; the gift was delivered as planned.'

'All is *not* fine,' I replied. 'I had another letter last night. It was dropped off while I was at the mansion. Ilona found it. This time it was written in invisible ink.' When I told him that whoever wrote it wanted another rendezvous, he looked at Mustafa, who was shaking his head in disbelief.

'Of course, you must go,' Sam said.

'Of course – and possibly get murdered.'

Sam looked annoyed. 'Don't be so melodramatic, Elliot. It doesn't suit you.'

I was offended by his off-handedness, but what was the use arguing? 'Ilona wants to tail me, just in case.'

'Out of the question, dear chap. I will get someone else to tail you – someone who knows how to kill if necessary.'

'*I* know how to kill.' My reply was sarcastic. 'I'll carry a gun.'

'Elliot, I know perfectly well you know how to kill. That's not what I'm worried about. You are a foreigner and we have people who can tail you who will blend in well.' He looked at Mustafa. 'Isn't that right?'

A brief and spirited conversation took place in Turkish between the two of them, and after it was finished, Sam said that Mustafa has a few "trustworthy" friends he would call upon who were pro-Allies. One of them would tail me.

'Leave it to me,' Sam said. 'You just make sure you're on time.' Then he changed his mind. 'No. Make it ten minutes earlier. Buy a packet of cigarettes from a nearby vendor, then...'

'Then what?'

There was another short conversation between the two of them and Sam put his hand on my shoulder in a reassuring manner. 'There will be a cigarette vendor a few metres away from the cafe. Stop and buy a packet and ask how his children are. It will be your code and he will reply. If all is well, he will tell you they are fine. If he spots anything untoward, he will warn you with "All is not well", in which case you must leave as quickly as possible without attracting attention. Rest assured, we will have you covered.'

If that was meant to reassure me, it didn't, but I had no other option.

'And another thing,' Sam said. 'No more discussing this with Ilona. She's about to go back to Hungary and we don't want her compromised. You are too close. Besides, she has work at the club and we don't want Boris to become suspicious.'

Although I agreed, I was bitterly disappointed as she was one of the few people I trusted. She had good instincts. Sam noticed my disappointment. 'Not a word – okay.' He even went as far as saying I should lie to her. 'Tell her I am handling it.'

Mustafa excused himself as he had an appointment with a client. 'Stay here as long as you like. You're quite safe.'

When we were alone, I brought up the subject of Füsun. 'Did you know they've sent her away? An arranged marriage to someone utterly unsuitable. It was all so sudden.'

Sam laughed. 'I saw the way Füsun used to look at you. It was obvious she liked you and I suspect her father noticed too.'

'Then why did he send her to my apartment with a message?'

'Probably to test her out and see what would happen between the two of you.'

'That's not funny. You know, she even wanted to make love, but I refused. In fact she almost threw herself at me. I couldn't understand what got into her. She'd always acted so... so shy and pious.'

'How long have you been here?' Sam replied with a heavy sigh. 'Almost six months and you still don't know the Turkish ways. Her father would probably have killed you both if you had. Whatever transpired – thankfully, nothing – he obviously sensed her feelings. Leave well alone, Elliot. As you say, she may be entering an unsuitable marriage, but it is not up to us to interfere. If I were you, I would not bring up her name again. You are lucky her father thinks you're an honourable man.'

I could tell this was a warning I had better heed. The last person I wanted to cross was Mustafa. God knows what he was capable of with that curved knife he carried in his cummerbund.

'I have some other news I think you should know,' Sam said, pouring himself another cup of tea. 'This may come as a surprise, but von Papen has had a secret meeting with us – OSS. It's not the first time he's done this. His first approach was in summer, but he's reached out again. Naturally, he won't go through diplomatic channels for fear of it being leaked. He says he realises the war is lost and has greatly exaggerated his influence in Germany. He's asked for US support to make him in charge of a post-Hitler Germany. Of course, all this was told to Allen Dulles, who confided in President Roosevelt. Naturally, the offer has been rejected and we have been ordered to desist talking to him about the subject. The Americans have a long memory when it comes to von Papen. They have not forgotten how he abused his diplomatic immunity as German military attaché in 1914, violating US laws to start organising plans for incursions into Canada for a campaign of sabotage against canals, bridges and railroads. He was also covertly arranging arms with Indian nationalists based in California for a planned uprising against the British in India. Fortunately for him, his diplomatic immunity protected him from arrest. In 1915, the US government declared him persona non grata and he was recalled to Germany. Of course your lot – British intelligence – know all about all this, so we are hardly likely to take him seriously.

'The thing is, we believe that somehow von Papen and the German embassy have gained access to important information which could only have come from the Tehran Conference, as he is revealing selective information to Inönu to strain Allied-Turkish relations. As a German, and particularly an ardent Nazi, although he has professed otherwise to us, he could not gain secretive information without there being a spy in our ranks.'

I could hardly believe my ears. This was worrying news, especially for our assignment. I knew von Papen was not to be trusted, but that also went for many other people I'd met during this war who would sell their souls to the highest bidder.

'What if all this was leaked to Hitler?' I asked. 'That would set the cat among the pigeons.'

'It would, but then Hitler might replace him with someone far more dedicated to the Nazi cause and less eager to save his own neck.' Sam went quiet for a moment. 'Von Papen may have helped bring Hitler to power, but Hitler is no fan of von Papen. As soon as he no longer needed him, Hitler and his allies marginalised von Papen. He would be shot for treason if Hitler got wind of it. Göring, in particular, despises him.'

'You seem to know an awful lot,' I said.

'We have our informants just as he does, but in this case, the international press reported on the real turning point of his demise. Von Papen obviously intended to "tame" Hitler. Two weeks after the University of Marburg speech, in which von Papen called for the restoration of certain freedoms, demanded an end to the calls for a "second revolution", and advocated the cessation of SA terror in the streets, Hitler responded to the demands of the armed forces and the ambitions of Ernst Röhm and the SA by purging the leadership during the Night of the Long Knives. Von Papen was placed under house arrest at his villa with his telephone line cut. Some accounts indicate that this "protective custody" was ordered by Göring. Whoever it was, von Papen understood he was no longer a member of the inner circle and naively demanded a private audience with Hitler. Word has it that he announced his resignation, stating, "My service to the Fatherland is over!" His resignation as vice-chancellor of the party was accepted with no successor appointed.'

'Then he was sent here?'

'Not until after Hitler made him the German ambassador to Vienna and gave him assignments working with Mussolini and the Hungarian prime minister. Let's not forget that he may no longer be one of the inner circle, but he is still a nationalist. Von Papen came here in 1939 after the retirement of the previous ambassador, Frederich von Keller. Foreign minister Joachim von Ribbentrop attempted to appoint him as ambassador in Ankara, but the appointment was vetoed by Mustafa Kemal, who, like the Americans, remembered von Papen well and with considerable distaste: he had served alongside him in World War I. For someone working in the field of diplomacy, he makes quite a few enemies.'

Why all of this information about von Papen, much of which I already knew, I asked myself, but Sam continued.

'General İnönü, when he became president, again vetoed Ribbentrop's attempts to have von Papen appointed as German ambassador to Turkey, but a few months later accepted him. Von Papen arrived in Turkey in April 1939, just after the signing of a UK-Turkish declaration of friendship. İnönü wanted Turkey to join the UK-inspired "peace front" as that was meant to thwart Germany's ambitions. France and Turkey also signed a declaration committing them to upholding collective security in the Balkans. However, some months later, von Papen threatened Turkey with economic sanctions and the cancellation of all arms contracts if she did not cease discussions with the UK and France. Naturally, this was a threat that Turkey rebuffed.

'Our sources informed us that when he heard the news of the German attack on Poland, he was deeply depressed but continued his work of representing the Reich in Turkey. It was he who signed the agreement with Turkey in June 1941, preventing her from entering the war on the Allied side.'

'We are dealing with a slippery eel,' I replied. 'One who will change sides to suit himself.'

'Indeed, and it's not unusual for him to hold parties at the German embassy attended by leading Turkish politicians purportedly using "special funds" to bribe Turks into following a pro-German line.'

'Do you think that's what he was doing last night?'

'As far as we know, Kulin is with neither side. He is an industrialist and will accommodate the government's wishes to keep his status. No, I think Kulin is far too smart. He knows he must survive after the war has finished.

'Sorry. I got carried away. What I wanted to say was that there were other Germans there last night – fresh faces. You probably wouldn't have noticed, but I did. I've been here longer than you. The Reich must have sent more Gestapo agents looking to infiltrate everyone and everything.'

'You mean von Papen too?'

'Highly likely, but the ones I am really am worried about are Messner and Issakides. We already know that *all* members of the Reich are being watched, particularly those who travel freely, and they are aware they are under close scrutiny, but I believe the situation has worsened even more than they realise. Collaborators will be dealt with swiftly. You know that.'

'So you think the man who was murdered was a collaborator?'

'Not necessarily. I think the least the Gestapo would do was interrogate someone first and that man didn't appear to have been tortured. Quite the opposite.'

'Where are you getting all this information from?' I asked. 'And why are you telling me now?'

'I'm limited as to what I can say, but it comes from intelligence and reports in the field. I think the man who was shot worked for the Gestapo and whoever saw him knew this. I don't think those bullets were meant for you.'

'Well, that's a relief.' My tone was more than a little sarcastic as his words were not at all reassuring. In fact, I think he was trying to reassure himself rather than me.

'There's something else, Elliot. There was a man with Messner and von Papen last night whose face was familiar. I had the worrying feeling I'd seen him somewhere before but couldn't think where.'

'Austrian? German? Diplomat – or Secret Police?'

'I don't know. I didn't get close enough to hear the accent except to learn that they were speaking German. Messner seemed to know him.'

'Will you get chance to see Messner before he leaves? Maybe you could ask him.'

'Annoyingly, I only got notice of his arrival the day before he arrived – a coded message from OSS in Cairo. They didn't say anything other than we were to hand over the money and that Messner would be here for two days. Issakides goes on to Sofia; he goes back to Vienna.' Sam rubbed his temple. 'I will try my utmost to make contact before he leaves.'

'If you do, will you tell him about the man who was shot?'

'You mean the well-dressed man from Vienna? No. I don't think it's wise to worry him unnecessarily when we know nothing about the man.'

The normally urbane, world-wise, and unflappable Sam seemed to display more than a hint of anxiousness, but I didn't pursue it.

'A slight change of plan,' he said suddenly. 'On second thoughts, to be on the safe side, meet me in the bar at Sirkeci Station about an hour before your meeting, just in case I can pick up any more information that could be of help.' He looked at his watch. 'Now, I really must get a move on. I have a lot to do today.'

We left the han together. He went into the Grand Bazaar and I turned left, passing by the Büyük Valide Han, to browse in a couple of bookstores. This area around the Grand Bazaar was filled with hans, almost all of them dating back centuries to the heyday of the Ottoman Empire when the only mode of transport along the silk road were the camel trains. The narrow cobblestoned road curved downwards, past a myriad of small shops and tiny cafes, barely large enough to sit more than half a dozen people, towards the Egyptian Spice Bazaar. Here the streets were even narrower. Ilona was right. It was a maze where one could get lost even with a map. I wanted to check the area out, particularly the spot where the meeting was to take place. With so many people about, buying fresh coffee, vegetables, and spices, or partaking in a warm glass of salep or boza from a passing vendor, I blended in with the crowds. It would be quite a different matter after midnight.

CHAPTER 5

ILONA, CLAD IN a peach-coloured satin bra and a narrow girdle over her panties, was in the bedroom laying out evening gowns on the bed. 'I can't decide what to wear,' she said with a frown. 'Help me choose?'

The last thing I needed was this. 'I prefer you as you are,' I said, reaching for the whisky bottle. 'Half-naked!'

She threw me a concerned look. 'My, my! Have you had a bad day? It's a bit early for that, isn't it?'

When I didn't answer she folded her arms and looked at me sternly. 'What's happening? Did you see Sam?'

'I did and it's all taken care of.'

'What's that supposed to mean?' Her voice was sharp, tinged with heavy sarcasm.

'Exactly what I said.' I wasn't in the mood for an inquisition. 'Sam is looking into the mystery man himself and he wants me to stay out of it.' I took a large gulp of whisky while she scrutinized me, allowing me to let off a little steam. I took two magazines out of a paper bag and gave them to her. 'I called by the bookstore and bought these for you. The latest edition of *Modenschau* and another *Yildiz* – one that features Hollywood films and film stars. This one has Greta Garbo in it.'

She sat on her chair in front of the dressing table and glanced through them, noting the most glamorous clothes. 'That's very thoughtful. Thank you.' After a few minutes, she got up and continued choosing her dress for the evening.

I drank my whisky while reading the newspaper, but it was hard to concentrate. 'What did you do after I left?' I asked.

'I went for a little pampering at the Çemberlitaş Hammam with Mathilde. The architecture is quite extraordinary – it's astounding to think it's so old. There is also something quite special about having an invigorating yet relaxing massage on the heated marble slab while looking up at the slender rays of sunlight beaming down from the star-shaped oculi in its magnificent dome.'

'I agree. It's one thing I will miss when I leave. Public baths have been an integral part of this the region for thousands of years. Any self-respecting Roman city would have had a large and, I imagine, beautiful bath at its heart. Even the Greeks had bathhouses.'

'Possibly, but here, Turkish cleanliness goes hand in hand with Islamic beliefs.'

'I believe you have them in Budapest too.'

'Yes, and many thermal baths. I used to go with my parents when I was a young girl. It was a special treat.' I wondered if she would go when she returned in a few weeks' time. She hummed a Hungarian tango while she looked at the gowns strewn on the bed, then picked up a rose-blush satin halter-neck dress and placed it against her body. 'Yes, this is the one. I will wear it with a diamond and ruby brooch. Do you agree?'

She stood there waiting for my answer while I tried desperately to hold back my anger at her idle chit-chat.

'I see,' she said in an off-handed manner. 'You are in one of your moods. In that case, I shall not bother you again until you've returned to your usual pleasant self.' She threw the dress down on the bed and went back to the dressing table to paint her nails.

'For goodness sake, Ilona, I have so much on my mind and all you can do is prattle on about a dress! What's the big deal, anyway? You know you look good in all of them. You don't need my opinion.' I found myself shaking. 'Why all the fuss? Is someone special going to the club tonight – another lover maybe? You've been acting strangely, disappearing with Sam...'

She picked up a small jar, turned around, and threw it at me with such force that if I hadn't ducked, it would have knocked me out. Instead it hit the wall and shattered, smearing the wall and floor in thick white face cream. At the same time she hurled abuse at me in Hungarian. I realised I had overstepped the mark.

'Édesem, forgive me.'

'*Utállak. Menj innen!*' To make it clearer, she said it in English. 'I hate you. Go away!'

I pulled her up roughly and held her close as she struggled and pummelled at me, trying to free herself. 'Go to hell,' she screamed.

There was a banging on the door and a woman's voice called out in Turkish. 'Is everything alright?'

'All is fine,' I shouted out. 'I dropped a plate.'

We heard her footsteps as she retreated down the hallway, mumbling something to herself about foreigners.

My attention returned to Ilona. 'I'm sorry. Please forgive me. You know I didn't mean to hurt you.'

Tears streaked her face. 'I know you have a lot on your mind, but do you think you are the only one who is worried?'

I held her tightly without uttering a word. After a few minutes, we kissed and the anger subsided, replaced by a quiet understanding. The strain was getting to us both and we needed to stay calm. I cleaned up the mess on the floor and wall and returned to the kitchen while she continued getting dressed. When she was ready, she came out and asked me how she looked. I took both her hands kissed them, telling her she was the most beautiful woman I'd ever known.

'I realise both you and Sam are trying to protect me,' she said in a soft voice, 'and for that I am grateful, but the fact of the matter is that I too am involved with OSS. What affects you two also affects me.'

'It's simply a case of keeping you safe, my love. We don't want anything to jeopardise your assignment when you return to Budapest. Now please, let's not fight about it. Just accept this is the way it has to be.'

'I wanted to let you know that Boris said he has a group of important customers tonight –Germans. He told me von Papen's secretary made the booking and said we were to look after them well.'

I pricked up my ears. 'Germans?'

She shrugged. 'People from the Reich, I presume. I will do what I can to find out who they are.' She paused for a moment. '*And* I promise to behave myself. What will you do with yourself?'

I just shook my head and remained silent. She knew I couldn't tell her.

She picked up her fur stole. 'Whatever you do, be careful,' she said with a half-smile. 'And when I come home, we can make love.'

The apartment felt empty and soulless after she left. Our happiness had been replaced by a cloud of despair and I hated myself for lying to her and brushing her off like that. The truth was that I didn't know what I'd do if something happened to her, but Sam was right. We had to keep her out of this. What she was about to do was extremely dangerous. If she was caught passing money to the Austrian resistance in Budapest, she would be tortured and killed. The thought sickened me and for that reason alone, we had to find out what was going on with this mystery man. I checked my gun and, just to be on the safe side, slipped my knife into one of my socks. The Colt M1903 that Sam had issued me with when I first arrived was one of the best compact pistols on the market. It offered excellent reliability and was easy to conceal. Its light weight and small size were a gift to a man like me who wasn't trying to get into a gunfight but to gather intelligence. I had been used to other guns but this suited me fine. I only hoped I wouldn't have to use it.

*

The bar at Sirkeci Station was full, mostly with people waiting to take the train to Bulgaria. I spotted Sam reading a newspaper in the corner of the room next to a warm heater.

'All set to go?' he asked after he requested the waiter to bring me a glass of wine.

I nodded.

'What did you tell Ilona?'

'As we agreed: that you were taking care of it.'

'Did she believe you?'

'You know Ilona. I don't think so, but I did my best to assure her. She told me that Boris said von Papen's secretary made a booking for a group of his friends tonight. Germans. I wonder why they are going there when their preferred venue is the Orient Club?'

'Interesting. I have some other news for you. I met with another one of our group. He told me that he received a message from Messner that he wanted to see me, but he was aware the Gestapo are watching him. I sent a message back reassuring him that we were doing our utmost to be careful and will work out a time and place.' We drank our wine in silence, watching the passengers board the late night express.

I looked at the clock on the wall. I had just fifteen minutes to get there. 'I'd best be off then,' I said.

'I'll be here for a while,' Sam said. 'After that you can reach me at the bar in Fener. Otherwise, we'll meet up tomorrow at Mustafa's. Good luck.'

When I left, the platform was filled with foreign diplomats and people waving their friends off. There was a piercing whistle, the engine emitted a huge cloud of steam, and slowly the train started to pull out of the station. It wasn't a long walk to my destination and I was there five minutes early. The narrow streets were eerily dark – with the occasional light coming from a dimly lit street lamp, a bar, or the slits in the closed shutters of small apartments over the shops –and there was hardly anyone around, but that didn't mean I wasn't being watched. It was like walking through a city of shadows. As I neared Ismail's cafe, I saw the cigarette vendor, sauntered up to him, and bought a packet.

'How are you children?' I asked. He replied that they were well. Then he walked away, calling out every now and again, '*Sigaralar*. Cigarettes. The finest Turkish tobacco.'

I put my hand in my pocket as I walked past the cafe first, noting who was inside. The Colt was reassuring. The cafe was typical of many in the area: barely large enough to hold half a dozen small tables with a narrow bar at the far end, a large samovar on the bar top, and an assortment of bottles, most of them raki. Two young men in their twenties were sitting at one table playing backgammon, a middle-aged man reading a newspaper was at another, and an old man smoking a narghile was in the corner. The two men finished their game and got up to leave. My heart pounded in my chest. I hadn't thought of *two* men. I sauntered away in the direction of the Egyptian Bazaar and stood in the recess of a shop doorway, leaning against its firmly locked shutters. Nearby, a cat screeched and ran across the street after a rat. The two men walked away in the opposite direction without seeing me. Obviously they had nothing to do with my meeting.

By now, the only people in the street were a couple of old men carrying large sacks on their backs who headed in my direction and fortunately walked straight past without even glancing at me, as if it was commonplace for people to lurk in the shadowy recesses of doorways. That left two men in the cafe. Surely the mystery man must be the one reading the newspaper? An old man smoking a narghile didn't fit into my imagination. Nothing seemed to be happening, and I wondered if I wasn't being sent on a wild goose chase. But I knew better – danger lurked among the most seemingly mundane places and appeared when you least expected it.

I looked at my watch. It was now five minutes past twelve, and the old man also got up to leave. He stood in the doorway leaning on a crutch and looked left and right before walking away. Was he looking out for me? As he walked I noticed that his left leg seemed paralysed. It occurred to me that it might even be a disguise as I'd occasionally resorted to that sort of thing at one time or another in the field. Being an actor was a prerequisite for being an agent. But no; he hobbled past me, and like the two old men, took no notice of me at all. When he turned the corner and didn't reappear, I concluded that he was not the mystery man.

It was now fifteen minutes past twelve, and there was only one man left in the cafe. I decided he must be the contact, but why hadn't he come for me? It was a dilemma. As a secret agent, I was told not to wait more than five minutes after the time specified – ten minutes at the most. But at fifteen minutes now – well, that was throwing caution to the wind, so I decided to leave. If the man saw me and he *was* the mystery man, then he would come after me. At that moment a young boy came around the corner bouncing a ball with one hand and carrying a large shopping bag in the other. He couldn't have been much older than twelve or thirteen and was shabbily dressed, but after several months in Istanbul, I was used to such poor ragamuffins out at night bartering something or other for a day's food or running errands for their poor families. They reminded me of a scene out of a Dickens novel. The boy had a small dog with him. As I moved away, the boy called out – 'Caldwell Bey!'

I swung around. 'Are you Caldwell Bey?' he asked again in broken English.

'Why?' The dog started yapping at my ankles and he gave it a swift kick.

'Answer me.' The dog gave a low menacing growl, spittle coming from its mouth as if it was about to set upon me.

'Yes.'

He fished inside the large bag, which appeared to be full of vegetables, and took out an envelope. 'This is for you.'

With that he walked away, bouncing his ball with the mangy dog following closely behind.

Was that it, I asked myself as I put the envelope in my inside overcoat pocket. The cafe was still open and I saw that the last customer – the middle-aged man – was paying the waiter. He caught my eye as I passed. Something made me think he knew what had just taken place. I turned out of Tahmis Sokak into Hasircilar Street, my hand still on my gun, and kept looking behind me to see if he was following. He wasn't, but something made me turn back. When I rounded the corner, the cafe was closed and the lights were off. The place was in darkness yet the man stood there, hiding in the shadows as I had done earlier, except that he was smoking a cigarette. I took my cigarettes out of my pocket and, in Turkish, asked if he had a light.

Without uttering a word, he struck a match for me while I held the cigarette in my mouth. In the semi-darkness, I took a good look at him. It was now or never.

'What do you want?' I asked.

'You have the envelope?'

'Yes. Who are you?'

'That's all I can say. I am trying to warn you. Be careful.'

With that he hurried away. 'Don't follow me,' he called out. 'Go home.'

Something told me not to confront him but to heed his words, and I quickly walked back towards Hasircilar Caddesi again. I had only gone a few metres when I thought I heard a gunshot. The area was filled with strange sounds of the night, but I was definitely sure this was a gunshot.

I immediately ran back to Tahmis Sokak. Other people must have heard something too because several lights went on in the upstairs windows, and a couple of people came out of previously locked narrow doorways and ran around the corner into one of the small lanes towards the far end of the street. Throwing caution to the wind, I decided to follow them and take a look. By the time I got there, a small crowd had gathered around a body lying on the cobblestones. I edged my way through to take a closer look and my heart missed a beat. It was the man in the cafe, and from what I could see, it looked as if he had been shot at close range in the head. To make matters worse, the boy with the ball and dog was walking towards us. His dog ran ahead, yapping at my ankles again. By now people were coming from nowhere, whereas only twenty minutes earlier, the area had been almost deserted. I was scared that the boy might point me out as a suspect. I had to get away before people realised I was a foreigner and fingers pointed at me. After all, I *was* carrying a gun and could be easily blamed.

I hurried away, taking a different way out of the area, back towards Sirkeci, where I found a bar filled with people where I would blend in. I ordered a raki to calm my nerves while I thought of what to do next. I knew I should go and tell Sam, but what would I say? That I was in the vicinity of yet another suspicious murder? This was turning into a nightmare. At least I still had the envelope. I drank my raki and decided to get a taxi back to my apartment.

The apartment was in darkness. Thankfully Ilona was still at the Rose Noir. I quickly opened the envelope and to my astonishment found what looked to be a handwritten shopping list: coffee; tea; biscuit; dried beans; vegetables, and much more. I stared at it for a few minutes and then realised it must be coded, but none of it made any sense. Then it dawned on me that perhaps the message would be in invisible ink again. I held it to the hot lamp and sure enough, a few words began to show in the spaces between the lines. They were names. *Alfred Schwarz, Sigismund Roman, Laufer, Hatz.* The last few words sent shivers down my spine. They read: *Semperit Rubber infiltrated.* I checked several times just to make sure there was no mistake. Who were these people? I had to let Sam know straight away.

I put the note in my pocket along with my gun and made my way to Fener. By now it was almost three o'clock in the morning. The bar was closed and in darkness, but after knocking several times, Ilios came and let me in. He took me upstairs to their living quarters, where Sam was sleeping on a makeshift couch in the kitchen.

'What's happened,' he said, his eyes widening when he saw the look on my face. 'Did something go wrong?'

I told him what took place and about the names. He shook his head. 'Schwarz... Where have I heard that name before?' Then he hit his head with the palm of his hand. 'He's one of us – an Austrian employed by OSS. McFarland appointed him. He's known by another name.'

I couldn't believe my ears. Lanning 'Packy' Macfarland was head of OSS Istanbul. I'd met him once before and didn't take a shine to him. He didn't seem as competent as Dulles, or Sam for that matter, but he was the one responsible for hiring agents connected with the various assignments in Istanbul, especially the Austrian resistance.

'What if we have a double agent in our midst?' Sam looked worried and I could tell he was relieved we'd kept everything to ourselves until now.

'Leave it to me,' he said. 'I'm going to make some enquiries. Messner leaves today. I would like to see him but I don't know if it's possible. I am sure that if he suspected something was wrong he would have let us know, and I don't want to worry him unnecessarily. I thought all was going well.'

He told me to go back home and not to breathe a word about any of this to Ilona. 'One good thing,' he said as I got up leave, 'at least the murderer wasn't after you.'

Like the last time, it didn't make me feel any better. In fact I felt worse. Two men were dead and I had been at the scene on both occasions.

CHAPTER 6

IT WAS ALMOST dawn when I returned home and, in order not to disturb Ilona, who was fast asleep, I slept on the couch. When I woke in the morning she was listening to the radio in the kitchen and flicking through the magazines. The smell of coffee, perfume, and stale cigarettes permeated the apartment.

'I came home expecting us to make love,' she said in her sultry voice as she spread mulberry jam onto her bread, 'but as you weren't here...'

'I decided to go and play cards in Fener.' My reply was curt and I don't think she believed me.

'So what are you doing today?'

'Nothing much – maybe catch up with Sam, go for a long walk.' She finished her breakfast, took my cigarette from me, stubbed it in the overflowing ashtray, and led me back into the bedroom. No words passed between us, but we made love and lay in each other's arms until lunchtime. After that, I felt more relaxed.

'Let's go for one of those fish meals down by the Bosphorus,' Ilona said. 'The weather has cleared up again.'

Clad in our winter clothes, we walked arm in arm and sat at one of the rickety wooden tables and ordered a fish sandwich. The place was filled to capacity. Not even the weather could stop the Istanbulite from indulging in one of their favourite meals – freshly caught fish and fried on the spot.

I asked her how it went with the Germans.

Ilona wiped her mouth with a paper napkin and grinned. 'I wondered when you would get around to that. I sang a few of their favourite songs, danced the foxtrot and tango with a couple, and otherwise, quite enjoyed myself. Politics was not discussed, at least not in my presence.' She paused for a moment while she finished her sandwich. 'You're not jealous, are you?' I didn't answer.

'The group turned out to be a mix of Germans, Austrians, and four Hungarians. Myself and one of the Hungarian girls, Rozsika, made small talk in Hungarian and we made sure they spent big – cigars, fine wines, caviar. Boris was most impressed. The Hungarians, in particular, seemed in a nostalgic mood, probably due to the drink, and I was asked to sing a few favourites. For that they tipped handsomely. A thousand Reichsmark – real money! Not bad for a few songs and a little chit-chat about our homeland.'

'I suppose that will go towards your villa in the country after the war?' I was a little facetious but immensely happy she hadn't slept with one of them for the money.

'I did have my eye on an embroidered kaftan in the Grand Bazaar, but will resist the urge. Yes, it will go towards the villa.' She laughed. 'Who knows, you may even come and visit me one day. That is, of course, if you haven't settled back into English country life – and Dorothy will allow you.'

This time it was she who was being facetious. I reached for her hand. 'Wherever you are, I will find you again, remember that. It might take time, but you won't get rid of me that easily.'

She raised an eyebrow and gave a knowing smile. 'We will all be changed people after the war.' She was right as usual. It wasn't wise to think that far ahead. 'Anyway,' she said, 'enough of this small talk. I did something that will make you *very* happy. I got Rozsika to take a photograph of us all – when Boris wasn't looking, of course. She'll give it to me tonight after it's been developed.'

Now this was good news: dangerous, but I appreciated it very much. What she said next was even better.

'I found out two of the Hungarians' names.'

By now I was hanging on to every word. 'Go on.'

'Otto Hatz and Lothar Kovass.'

I felt the blood drain from my face.

'What's wrong? Do you know them?'

I knew I had to be careful and tried to sound a little casual. 'I've heard one of those names somewhere before. I'll check them out.'

Ilona eyed me with suspicion. 'You *think*? It's not like you to forget names.'

'Hungarian names are harder to remember than French, German, or British.'

'I would have thought it was the opposite,' she replied. 'It's precisely because they are different that you remember them.'

'I'll know when I see the photograph. Did they say what they were doing here?'

'A few seemed to be here working as they knew a few Turkish words. The others were visiting.'

'You don't know what this means to me.'

She brushed her hand through her hair. 'I think I do, édesem, so you owe me.' She changed the subject. 'I've enjoyed myself today. It makes a change to get out for a while. We should do it again soon – before I go back to Budapest. Maybe we could take a ferry to the Asian side.'

'I'd like that. Now, what will you have for dessert?'

Ilona patted her belly. 'Are you trying to fatten me up?'

'Not at all: I like you just the way you are.'

I decided to go and see Sam after I'd seen the photograph. That meant an agonising wait until I picked it up from Ilona at the Rose Noir later that evening. Not wanting to seem overly anxious, I spent a quiet afternoon in the apartment with her, reading or listening to music until it was time for Ilona to leave. She left just before seven. All day, the two murders, the names on the message, and their connections to the two Hungarians at the Rose Noir had been racing through my mind until I thought my head would burst. It was like trying to piece together a jigsaw with the most important pieces missing. Sooner or later it would fall in place – if I lived that long.

I was one of the first to arrive at the nightclub and was given the usual warm welcome by Boris, who showed me to a discreet table for two not far from the stage. An etched Art Deco inspired glass divider separated me from the couple behind, who spoke Romanian. I did not know any Romanian beyond a few basic sentences and words of love, the latter of which I had never had the occasion to use. But from what I could tell, the couple were in love and certainly making the best of their time alone, kissing and holding hands. He had his back to me, but I caught a glimpse of her, a stunning beauty with shoulder-length dark hair and dark eyes. I thought of the Russian folksong, "Dark Eyes". Ilona sometimes hummed it to herself in the apartment.

I ordered an excellent, perfectly chilled vodka, one that was hard to come by these days except by someone like Boris. It was accompanied by a bowl of Beluga caviar which came in a small glass dish that nestled inside a larger ornate silver platter containing ice. It was served with finger-length pieces of toast, toasted to exactly the right colour. I savoured the taste while I watched the warm-up act, a French jazz band with a vivacious, dark-skinned singer called Belle, who had a cheeky smile and flashing eyes. She reminded me of Josephine Baker, who I had once seen in Paris with my friend, Ernest Hemingway. I recalled him saying at the time that she was "the most sensational woman anyone had ever seen." Seeing them took me back to Paris. They were happy memories until the Germans marched in. Then it all changed. Those memories reminded me of why I was here, fighting this war.

After a short interval the curtains drew back to reveal the Budapest Gypsy Band, who played a few a few musical numbers in which all the musician excelled, stirring the audience with their vitality and musical prowess before Ilona walked on stage. Everyone clapped loudly. She wore a red rose in the right side of her hair and was dressed in one of her sequined dresses that sparkled under the spotlight like the finest diamonds in a jeweller's window. After one or two moments, the violinist struck up a few melancholic chords, joined by the flute and lute, and Ilona began to sing, a beautiful, love song filled with pathos and passion. It was so haunting that it sent shivers down my spine.

I had learned so much about Hungarian gypsy music from Ilona during our time together. Its roots were wide, with influences reaching back to the East, especially the Tatar and Anatolian Turks, which she said was why it was so popular in Istanbul. Within a matter of seconds, the rhythm could race from soft to energetic. It was magical and, like Ilona herself, filled with passion and unpredictability. Ilona's flawless interpretation of a string of love songs was well-received. When she finished, she took a bow and the audience clapped enthusiastically for several minutes. As she blew them a kiss with both hands, the stage lights dimmed and the curtain closed. She had half an hour before the second part of the show and joined me at my table.

'How was I?' she asked as she took a cigarette from an ivory cigarette case given to her by an admirer. She put it between her lips, glistening with red lipstick, and leaned over for me to light it.

'Need you ask? You were wonderful.' I had long learned that despite her beauty and voice, she still needed reassurance and I was happy to oblige. 'Have you got it?' I asked in a hushed voice.

She took a long drag of her cigarette, then pulled an envelope from her bag and slid it across the table. 'There you are. I've marked the Hungarians.'

I slipped it in my pocket and did my utmost to enjoy the rest of the short time I was with her, but all I could think of was the photograph. When it was time for her second half, she put her hand over mine, reassuringly. 'Take care, Elliot.'

As soon as she'd gone I left the building and got a taxi home. In the privacy of the apartment, I pulled the photograph out of the envelope and took a good look at the faces. Ilona had written the initials of those she'd named just above their heads. O.H. for Otto Hatz and L.K. for Lothar Kovass. The other two Hungarians were marked with a cross. I stared at their faces for a while but didn't recognise anyone – except... Yes, the more I looked, the more I thought I recognised one of the Germans – or Austrians – but I couldn't recall from where. And then there was that name again – Otto Hatz – the same name mentioned in the last note. To say that I was disappointed I didn't know any of them was an understatement. It was time to meet with Sam again, but before that, and despite my better judgement, I decided to go back to the scene of the second crime and sniff around. Who knows what I what might uncover? It was worth a try.

Rather than wear the same black overcoat, I wore a different one, an old and rather heavy muddy brown-coloured one that I'd picked up for a bargain in the bazaar. I put my gun, along with the photograph, in the inside pocket, and my knife in my sock again, just in case. In all the time I'd been a secret agent, I'd never had cause to use the knife for anything more than opening locked doors and windows, but the gun – or *a* gun, not the one I had now – I had used, and far more times than I cared to remember, but never here in Istanbul.

I took a taxi to near the Rüstem Pasha Mosque and walked the rest of the way, retracing my steps as I had on the previous evening. By now it was almost 11:00 p.m. and both Hasircilar Caddesi and Tahmis Sokak were still fairly busy. Quite a few of the shops were still open, hoping to make a last-minute sale when times were hard. Ismail's cafe was open and half-filled with customers. This time I would not lurk in the shadows as before, but go in and have a quiet drink. Before I did that, I wanted to see where the man was shot. Thankfully there was enough light from nearby windows and a streetlamp for me to make out the blood stains still on the cobblestone. I stopped to take a good look, thinking perhaps he might have dropped something – some vital piece of evidence I could use that no one else had noticed – but no, there was nothing.

A rather large, middle-aged woman wearing a headscarf was watching me as she swept the litter from the pavement near her door. 'Are you a policeman?' she asked.

I thought quickly. If I said yes, I would get myself into trouble. 'No,' I replied. 'A friend told me someone was shot here last night.'

'That's right.'

'Do you know who the poor fellow was?'

The woman leaned on her broom and eyed me suspiciously. 'Why?'

'It's just that I was going to meet a friend and he didn't turn up.

78

I wondered – no – it's crazy really, but I wondered if it might be my friend.' I waved my hand through the air. 'A ridiculous thought; he was probably drinking in a bar somewhere and forgot about me.'

The woman's face hardened. 'You're a foreigner, aren't you?'

'I am, *Hanimefendi*, but a friend of Turkey.'

She shook her head. 'The police were here asking questions. We heard shots, but no one saw anything. That's all I can tell you. If you want to find out anything else, go to the police station. Inspector' – she thought for a few seconds – 'Aksoy, that's it. Inspector Aksoy, I think his name was. He was the man in charge.'

I thanked her and returned to the cafe. Aksoy, I thought to myself. I might have guessed he'd be sniffing around. I sat at a table near the window and ordered a raki. If the owner recognised me, he certainly didn't show it. Two men were playing backgammon at the next table. I mulled over the events in my mind. Everything seemed fine when the man selling cigarettes passed by. What happened to change things? Nothing seemed out of the ordinary in the cafe and I prepared to leave and head for Fener. Just as I was paying for my drink, I spotted the young boy with the ball walk past. He turned and saw me and then hastened away, with his mangy dog running after him. By the time I got outside, he'd gone. I followed in the direction I thought he was heading but couldn't see him. I looked in every doorway and nearby narrow laneways, of which there were many, and luckily caught sight of him disappearing into the blackness of a lane filled with rubbish, an alley so narrow, you could barely swing a cat around in it.

'Stop,' I called out, stepping on the stinking rubbish that littered the place. 'I mean you no harm. I just want to speak with you for a moment.'

The end of the alley was in complete darkness and I had no idea how far it was or whether it was a dead end. I dared not go any further and reached for my gun in case it was a trap. 'Please,' I said in a soft voice.

Then I heard the low growl of his dog. The boy must still be here. I was right. The dog charged out of the blackness and bit my ankle so hard that I swore as I tried to kick it away. 'Damn brute,' I called out, amongst other expletives while hitting it with my gun. As I tried to defend myself, the boy shot out of the darkness and ran past me towards the street.

'Stop,' I called after him, 'or I will shoot you and your dog.'

The boy refused to stop, skidding on the slippery rubbish as he ran away. I couldn't risk the noise of a shot and took the knife out of the sock, which thankfully was on the other foot. After one last attempt to shake the dog free, I had no other option but to stab the animal, fatally wounding it. On hearing its last agonising whimper, the boy momentarily stopped. The pain the dog had inflicted on me was agonizing, but filled with adrenalin, I managed to run towards the boy, who was now cowering beside a rubbish dump, and pulled him by the scruff of his jacket to me and held the bloodied knife at his throat.

'If you'd listened that wouldn't have happened. Now you and I will have a little chat.' I loosened my grip and, just to show I meant what I said, took out my gun, jabbing it in his chest. 'One scream, one false move and you meet the same fate as your wretched dog.' I pushed him back into the shadows.

The boy was trembling. 'Please put that gun away, efendi, I promise not to scream.'

I slid the gun inside my outer pocket but still kept the knife pointed at him. 'I want to know who that man was who gave you the note and why he was killed.'

'I had never seen him until that night,' he said, his eyes on the knife.

'I don't believe you.'

'It's true. I swear on the holy Koran.'

By now, my eyes were accustomed to the darkness and I could see the fear in his eyes. 'I said I don't believe you.' The timbre of my voice was menacing and I pushed the tip of the knife towards his throat. 'I will count to ten. After that you will end up like your dog. One, two, three...' When I reached eight, he'd still not said a word and I nicked his flesh with the knife, drawing blood. 'Eight, nine...'

His face grimaced with pain and, fearful that he would die, he changed his story. 'Alright. I'll tell you what I know, but it isn't much.'

'Go on. I'm listening.'

'The man pulled me aside a few hours before I met you and asked me to give you the letter. I asked what it was worth as I didn't want any trouble with the police. He described you and where you would be. He offered me a few liras and gave me half then and said I'd get the other half when I'd delivered it. I was warned that he would know if I'd delivered it.' Tears started to run down his cheeks. 'I knew he would be watching from that cafe. I'm not stupid, you know.'

'You didn't even want to know who this man was – after all, it's not every day you get paid good money for doing very little?'

'Why should I? It was easy money and I didn't care what was in the envelope.' He paused for a moment. 'Now let me go. I've told you all I can.'

'Not so fast. Where were you supposed to meet him to collect the rest of the money?'

'In the laneway where he was shot. I waited in the shadows – just as you were doing – and saw him coming towards me. I was about to jump out and ask for my money when another man hurried past and shot him. I didn't want anyone to think it was me so I ran away.'

'But you came back. I saw you.'

'Only after I knew people were coming out of the buildings to see what happened.'

'What did you tell the police?'

'I'm in enough trouble with the police as it is – petty thefts and the like. When the police turned up I was scared and ran off again.'

Something made me think he was telling me the truth and I moved back a little, lowering the knife.

His eyes narrowed. 'So, Caldwell Bey, are you going to pay me the remainder of the money I'm owed?'

He was young, but he had a ruthless streak and had played the innocence card well, yet all he cared about was his money. What's more, he knew my name.

'I don't owe you anything.'

He made a dash to get away from me, laughing that he would tell the police who I was – a foreigner called Caldwell. He was dangerous and I couldn't risk the police on my back. I *had* to kill him. Ignoring the agonizing pain from my ankle, I lunged at him and we fell on the ground in a scuffle where I stabbed him twice in the chest. His body jerked violently until he finally took his last breath. I jumped back up and hurriedly dragged him behind the rubbish dump, wiped my knife, and slid it back into the sock. Knocking over the rubbish had made a noise and I had to get away fast. Back in the street, I kept my distance behind a few people, making sure that I had no blood on my hands and face. Thankfully, any blood on the old overcoat wouldn't show.

Feeling utterly despondent at what had transpired, I went to see Sam in Fener.

CHAPTER 7

'Good Lord! What on earth happened?' Sam asked. 'You look a mess.'

Without waiting for an order, Ilios brought over the raki bottle and an extra glass, and a platter of olives, feta, and hard-boiled eggs. At the sight of the food, I nearly threw up. I put my gun on the table and took off my overcoat and inspected it. Blood had seeped into the lining. Thank goodness the muddy colour hid it the external stains. Ilios took it upstairs and asked his wife to clean it up. He came back with a clean set of clothes and told me to change. 'Marisa will wash everything for you,' he said. 'The coat is too thick, but she'll do what she can.'

When I took off my trousers and socks, I saw the state of my ankle. It was swollen and bleeding profusely. Sam quickly put a newspaper under my foot to stop the blood trickling into the carpet while Ilios ran back upstairs to fetch his wife.

She crossed herself when she saw the state of it. 'It needs cleaning straight away.' There was a sink in the room and she filled a large bowl with hot soapy water and brought it to me along with a towel. 'Here. Put your foot in this,' she said, pulling a stool up by my side and gently put my foot into it.

I tilted my head back in the chair, clenching my teeth. The water was hot. 'Bloody dog!' I said angrily and took another gulp of raki.

Sam and Ilios looked at each other. 'A dog!' said Sam with a broad grin on his face 'All this blood from a dog!'

I threw him a dirty look. If he was trying to be funny, his joke fell flat. 'I killed the damn thing.' I paused for a few seconds, cursing the pain as Marisa sponged the injury. 'Then I killed the boy.' I knew they wanted an explanation so I told them what transpired. Now that the drink had quelled my rage, I lapsed into despair at having killed a young boy.

'You did what you had to,' Sam said, matter-of-factly. 'He knew your name and, in all likelihood, would have thought he could get a few liras by going to the police and reporting you.'

'He was a street urchin killed in a knife fight. It happens all the time,' Ilios added in a similar tone. 'The police will probably not even bother to investigate.'

'He was a boy,' I replied miserably. I had tears in my eyes. 'I didn't sign up to kill young boys.'

Sam looked at me without pity. 'Get a grip on yourself. Ilios is right. Many people – old and young – get killed in knife fights. No one will suspect you.'

They were staring at me with emotionless expressions – the same expression I'd seen many times before on men used to dealing with danger and death. Then I sat up suddenly. 'The photograph!'

'What photograph?' Sam asked.

'That's the reason I came here in the first place – before all this.' I glanced at my ankle, which was turning a nasty bluish-purple. 'Ilona gave me a photo of a group of Hungarians, Germans, and Austrians taken at the Rose Noir. She marked some of them. It's in the inside pocket of the overcoat.'

Ilios ran upstairs to find it, returning with the envelope. 'Is this it?'

'Yes.' I pulled the photograph out of the envelope and handed it to Sam. 'Her friend took it while Boris was not around. Look here, she's marked a couple of them.' Sam peered at the faces for what seemed an eternity. 'Do you know any of them?' I asked.

Sam slumped down on the chair next to me. 'As a matter of fact, I do – one of them anyway. This doesn't look good.'

Ilios took the photo from him and also took a close look. 'Schwarz,' Sam said. Ilios nodded. He knew him too. 'This man here,' Sam added, tapping his finger on a man with a charming smile. 'That's Alfred Schwarz. The one I mentioned before – the Austrian businessman.'

Apart from the splashing of the water as Marisa cleaned my wounds, the room went silent as we processed this information, hoping there would be a plausible explanation.

'We can't keep this between ourselves any longer. I am going to see Macfarland tomorrow,' Sam said. 'He needs to know what's going on.'

As head of operations at OSS Istanbul, Macfarland, who was a banker from Chicago, maintained a cover story in Istanbul as a banker for the American lend-lease program. But as he himself had hired Alfred Schwarz, it would not reflect well on him if something was amiss. What we wanted to know now: was Schwarz at the Rose Noir with these people acting in our own interest, or was he a double agent?

'What about the Hungarians?' I asked. 'Hatz's name was in the secret message.'

'I am afraid I can't answer any more at the moment,' Sam replied. 'I need to show him the photograph. Do you mind if I take it?' I could hardly refuse as he was my handler. 'And remember – be careful what you say to Ilona. I don't want her involved,' he added. 'If she thinks something's amiss, she may pull out of her assignment.' I nodded. 'Good. Now, for the moment, I want you to lie low until I contact you again. It will also allow time for this injury to heal.'

Marisa took his foot out of the bowl, wiped it dry, and smeared ointment on the wound. 'We *could* find out who the dead man was by asking Inspector Aksoy. A woman who lived near the scene told me he was there after the murder. He might be able to help. We can always make up some excuse about looking for a friend who's gone missing.'

Ilios picked up the bottle and refilled my glass with the remaining raki while Sam sat back smoking a cigarette thinking about what to do next.

'Leave it to me,' he said. 'I'll come up with something. There's something else. I couldn't get to see Messner. We arranged to meet at a certain place along the Bosphorus. I would be sitting on a bench reading a book and he would sit next to me. The meeting was to take no more than five minutes. He turned up at the allocated time, but walked straight past. We locked eyes for a moment and I knew he was scared of approaching. He carried a rolled up newspaper, which he threw into a waste bin a few meters away from a salep vendor. I watched carefully and noticed two men following him at a safe distance – not safe enough for him not to realise they were Gestapo agents. I watched to see what would happen: would they retrieve the newspaper or not? They didn't. When they'd gone, I retrieved it, bought a glass of salep, and drank it on the bench, careful to see if I too was being watched. I wasn't and left for a safe location where I scanned the newspaper for any messages.' He paused for a moment, looking decidedly uncomfortable.

I listened attentively, wondering what would come next.

'At the bottom of one of the pages he had written a brief message saying one of his employees had gone missing – a man by the name of Steiner who worked in the accounts department.'

'And you think that might be the man who was trying to contact me?'

Sam gave a deep sigh. 'It's possible, but I have no idea what he looks like. Messner is now on a flight back to Vienna.'

It wasn't good news but at least it was something –a few more pieces to solve in this jigsaw of shady goings on. The attention turned back to my ankle. It didn't look good and they decided to call a doctor to check it out. With that, I was given a blanket and told to try and get some sleep.

In the morning I felt someone shaking me and woke up with a start, wondering where I was. 'The doctor's here to take a look at your ankle,' Ilios said. Marisa was with them but Sam had already left. The doctor was another Greek from Fener and they spoke in Greek as they examined the wound.

'Well, I think we can rule out rabies,' the doctor said. 'You would have shown signs of it by now and your temperature is fine. However, some of those bite marks are quite deep. A couple of stitches and you'll be fine.' He dabbed the area with a disinfectant, took out a needle and sterilized it in boiling water provided by Marisa, and set about suturing the worst parts. When he'd finished, he bandaged it and warned me to take care. 'Keep the leg up for a few days and the swelling should go down.'

I was given a bottle of pills and told to take two a day until they were finished. After another conversation in Greek, he left, refusing to take any money for his work.

'A good man,' Ilios said. 'He's one of us. We were lucky to catch him as he was just about to leave for a village on the Aegean coast opposite Samos. He helps the Greek resistants who are injured.' He handed me a clean pair of trousers, a shirt, and a woollen jumper, saying that Marisa had washed the others and I could pick them up another day. He suggested we burn the overcoat and I agreed. After what I'd done, I couldn't see myself wearing it again anyway.

Rather than let me catch a taxi, he took me back to my apartment in his car, for which I was grateful. The road leading to my apartment was barely wide enough for a car, with doorsteps that jutted out at irregular angles and uneven paving stones. I offered to get out and walk the rest of the way, but he wouldn't hear of it. When I got out, I saw Ilona's anxious face looking at me from the window.

'Keep out of trouble,' Ilios shouted after me with a cheeky grin before driving away.

'I've been worried sick,' Ilona said. 'What happened to you? Why are you limping?'

I slumped down into the chair and pulled up my trouser leg to show her the bandaged ankle. 'It's a long story and one that I don't want to talk about, except to say a dog attacked me on the way to see Sam.'

'A dog! Are you crazy?' She took a closer look and I could tell she knew there was more to the story. 'Will you be alright?'

'Yes, nothing that a few days off my feet won't mend. Sam's doctor fixed it up.'

'Why have you got new clothes? Did the dog tear your clothes to pieces too?'

I was not in the mood for her smart remarks. 'Will you stop asking questions?'

Exasperated, she put her hands on her hips and sighed heavily 'Fine.

No more questions. It seems that I can't ask you anything these days. Soon we will have nothing to talk about.' But her frustration soon dissolved and she bent down and wrapped her arms around me. 'I'm sorry, but I couldn't bear it if anything happened to you.'

I changed the subject and asked how her evening was to which she replied that it was uneventful. Uneventful was just what I needed to hear at that moment. She asked if I wanted breakfast but all I wanted was to sleep. The pills the doctor had given me were starting to kick in and I felt drowsy.

'I need to lie down and sleep for a while,' I said. 'I feel awful.'

Tenderly, she undressed me and lay down beside me in bed, snuggling up to me and comforting me with her soft kisses. Normally, I would be aroused, but within minutes I was fast asleep. When I woke up it was mid-afternoon and she was sitting in the chair opposite, reading a book.

'You've been asleep for almost six hours,' she said. 'Are you hungry? I'll fix you something to eat.' She didn't wait for me to reply and went to fetch a tray of delicacies with a glass of apple tea. 'How's your ankle?' she asked.

'The pain has subsided but it still throbs.' I reached for her hand. 'Sam took the photograph. He will check the men out.'

She didn't reply and for the first time there was a strange silence between us. It was as if we had come full circle – keeping our distance for a short while, then getting to know each other gradually, leading to a crescendo with such intensity that we almost burnt ourselves out – and now this. A strange silence was creeping into our relationship that I hoped would not tear us apart. I trusted her, but did she trust me? Both of us were here for a reason and we were powerless to respond. Powerless to act against the very organisation we worked for. There was nothing we could do but to let events take their course.

'Come here.' I drew her to me and we kissed with a passion, but it wasn't the same.

Then she giggled playfully, breaking the tension. 'Oh, my stallion, how can you mount me with your ankle like that?' She pushed me onto my back and I closed my eyes as she took charge. Skilled as she was in lovemaking, within minutes, I was aroused by her erotic touch and the warmth of her mouth on my skin. Like a sorceress casting aside demons, the pain from my ankle faded, replaced by the warm glow of ecstasy.

'There,' she said with a smile when it was over. 'Now you can go back to sleep again.'

CHAPTER 8

DUE TO A combination of the drugs the doctor had given me and an intense fever, I barely remembered the following few days. A lot can happen in a few days and it did. I was shocked. The first shock was that Ilona was leaving for Budapest in three days' time. It was Sam who told me this when he called at my apartment just as Ilona was leaving for the Rose Noir. I heard them whispering in the doorway as she left.

'What was that all about?' I asked.

'We've brought forward her assignment due to urgent requests from Messner. The Austrian resistance is desperate for more money. This was agreed from the top and relayed to us via Cairo.' Sam saw the look on my face and smiled. 'So, dear friend, it looks like you will be spending Christmas alone this year. No kissing under the mistletoe.' He never was one for a good joke and this one certainly fell flat.

His smile faded, replaced by one of his serious looks. He pulled up a chair and leaned forward with his hands clasped between his knees in a manner that reminded me of my childhood. My father adopted the same pose when he was about to give me one of his 'Look, son, it's like this', lectures after I'd misbehaved.

'I've seen Inspector Aksoy. I made an excuse about one of my men going missing. I gave him gave a fictitious name, of course, and said I wanted to file a missing person's report. He asked if I had a photograph and I produced this.'

He showed me an employment form with a black and white photograph in the right hand corner. It was one of the many OSS had faked. I'd had a few myself in my time. The name on the form read *David Pearson* and he was registered as *Executive Director – Philadelphia Import and Exports: A Division of Philadelphia Electrics, Inc, USA*. It was "officially" stamped by the Trade Department in Washington. The paper gave his date of birth as 1903. He had dark looks, a smooth complexion with a square jaw line, wore wire-rimmed glasses, and appeared to have light brown eyes. He was quite a handsome man, with no distinguishing features such as a scar or a birthmark, but he did have a moustache.

I felt a chill down my spine. 'You know, he looks remarkably similar to the man who gave me the envelope – but not quite. That man wore wire-rimmed glasses, but he didn't have a moustache.'

Sam gave a little half-smile. 'I was hoping you would say that.'

'Why's that?'

'Because we managed to get a photograph of the accountant who went missing from Semperit Rubber and searched through our files for a similar face. This man doesn't exist – well, at least not like this anyway.'

'So what are you trying to tell me?'

'We needed a look-alike and found someone who fitted the bill. I took this one to Inspector Aksoy at Sirkeci Emniyet Müdürlüğü and asked him if he knew anything about my missing business friend. Aksoy's reaction was similar to yours, except that he added a little more. "Hmmm, I think I know where your man is", he said. Of course, I tried to look relieved and asked if he'd been picked up for drunkenness and was in a cell.'

'Aksoy is an astute man. Didn't he suspect you were up to something?' I asked.

'If he did, he hid it very well. He opened his file and there among the top papers was the man you met. "His file is here, but the body is in the morgue. At least I think it is him. He wasn't carrying an ID." Naturally, I feigned surprise and great distress.'

I suppressed a smile. Sam was clearly enjoying this little game, despite the danger we were all in.

'When I asked what had happened, he told me that the man in

the file was found with two bullets to the head in a laneway near the Egyptian spice market and that they made a thorough examination of the scene where he was shot but no one saw anything. I told him there must be some sort of mistake. It must be someone else. Mr Pearson wouldn't be in an area like that.'

I nodded. 'And what did Aksoy say?'

'He fell for it. He asked me if I'd like to see the body so we could both make sure of his identity, and I agreed.'

'So what happened at the morgue?' I asked

'I was introduced to the head of forensics, a man called Kilic, who you're already acquainted with, and was taken to a room with several corpses. On the way, we passed a room where two more bodies were undergoing forensic investigation. When we reached the cold room, he told me there were about twenty bodies in storage: men and women of all ages. "Some have simply perished due to exposure in the cold weather and others had been killed in knife fights," Aksoy said, matter-of-factly.'

I felt a shiver down my spine recalling the poor boy I'd left in the alley. Sam saw the despondent look on my face, ignored it, and continued with his story. '"We even had a young teenager who had been stabbed in the heart," Aksoy continued. "Whoever did it must have known what he was doing as thankfully the poor boy would have died quickly." Has his family been notified, I asked innocently? He shook his head. "He was a street urchin – one of the many that roam the streets at night trying to make a living. They get themselves into mischief and end up dead. A notice has been put in the newspaper, but so far no one has claimed him".'

At the mention of the boy, I felt remorse again. The scene was still vivid in my mind and although I'd had had no other choice, I was still haunted by it, and probably would be for the rest of my life.

'Aksoy asked Kilic to remove a stretcher from one of the lockers. When the white sheet was pulled back, it revealed a corpse with two bullet holes to the head.'

By now, I was on the edge of my seat. 'Did you recognise him?'

'I did, and it took a great effort to hide it. It was Messner's accountant. Aksoy was watching me like a hawk, waiting for my reaction. I must have looked pretty awful as he asked Kilic to get me a glass of water. "Is this your man?" he asked. I told him no. "Take a good look," Aksoy said. "His face may look a little different in death."

'I turned away, wiped the sweat off my brow with a handkerchief, and apologised, saying that I was just relieved it wasn't my employee. I told him I was sure now that my friend must have had too much to drink and found a girl. Out of the blue, he asked about you. "How's that correspondent friend of yours – Caldwell Bey. It seems the two of you are always around when someone gets shot."'

'There you are,' I said. 'He must suspect something or he wouldn't have said that.'

Sam told me to calm down. 'I kept up my act and told him I had no idea what he was talking about. All I can say is that seeing the man in this state confirmed who it was that was trying to get in touch with you. Whoever killed him must have known he suspected a traitor in their midst.'

'But why come to me rather than tell Messner himself?'

'He would have known clandestine organisations such as OSS, SOE, and MI6 are operating here and probably wanted us to find out rather than go to Messner, who, in all likelihood, might have reacted badly. Remember, the employees are not privy to what he is doing and such a move could have put him in more danger. We don't know how he found this information.'

'But you said Messner knew he was being followed that day in the park.'

'Yes, but he would be aware that all citizens of the Reich who operate in neutral countries would be under suspicion. It's hardly new.'

We sat for a while, pondering the situation. It seemed that we might have come to a dead end. That's when the second surprise came.

'I went to see Macfarland and told him everything – the messages, the murders – and showed him the photograph taken at the Rose Noir.'

'What did he have to say?'

'He recognised Hatz and Laufer straight away and said they were "our men" recruited by Schwarz. His explanation as to why they were in such company was that they were probably keeping an eye on them in case there was anything to report back. "It's vital they maintain good relations with the Nazis," he said. In fact he was rather annoyed with me, adding that I was far too suspicious of everyone these days. He even went as far as saying I might need a holiday.'

I'd heard that sort of thing before. It was a euphemism for saying, if you don't mind your own business I will take you off the case and send you out of the country. 'So what did you do?' I asked.

'I stood my ground and told him I would sleep easier if we ran a few more routine checks on these men, especially Hatz and Laufer, rather than take Schwarz's word that they can be trusted. He narrowed his eyes and in no uncertain terms said he ran the network and not me. I was told to keep quiet in case Messner stopped supplying us with vital information. "We've already bombed important installations in Austria and Germany because we have his trust. It would pay you to remember that."'

'So the poor accountant lies in the morgue and we keep quiet.' It was a shocking thought, made even more shocking by the fact that Sam's boss told him to keep quiet.

Sam sat back in the chair and sighed. 'It's a dirty business, this spying game, isn't it? We knew that when we signed up. Anyway, enough of this, let's go and get something to eat. By the look of you, you could do with a good meal. Doesn't Ilona feed you?'

'Cooking is not really her forte.' I was somewhat irritated at the way he said it and put it down to being overly sensitive because I knew she was about to leave the country. 'Anyway, I haven't felt well enough to eat until now.'

'Well, Caldwell Bey, it's my treat. I know a good restaurant in Beşiktaş near the Dolmabahçe Palace so get dressed.'

Sam read the newspaper while I got ready. My trousers felt loose and I had to admit, he was right. I must have lost several kilos.

'By the way, how is the ankle?' Sam asked. I showed him. It was healing well. 'That doctor probably saved your leg, if not your life. You were lucky it didn't turn gangrenous.'

It wasn't everyday Sam treated me to a meal in a fine restaurant and

I looked forward to it. The establishment turned out to be one of the best in the city: well appointed and busy. We were greeted by the portly manager, who appeared to be on friendly terms with Sam, and given a table for two with an excellent view of the Bosphorus.

'We'll have a bottle of your finest red while we decide,' Sam said.

'I have just taken delivery of a few bottles from an excellent winery near Ankara made from Öküzgözü grapes,' the manager told us.

'Then we'll go with your recommendation.'

'What are Öküzgözü grapes?' I asked when we were alone.

'Dear me, Elliot, haven't you learned anything about wines since you've been here, or do you only drink raki? It's one of the oldest Turkish grape varieties, well suited to the Anatolian climate. Turkey is home to a multitude of indigenous wine grapes. Apparently, the first wineries were established in the early 1900s after a brief prohibition on the production, consumption, and sale of alcohol. As you know, Atatürk was not averse to a few drinks himself, and when the Turkish Republic was established, the ban was reversed. Lady Celia is a fan of Turkish wines herself. I'm surprised you haven't tasted them at one of her dinner parties.'

A bottle was brought to the table and Sam was given a little taste. It was a deep red colour. He tasted it like a man used to his wines and nodded. 'Perfect.' The man looked pleased and poured us both a glass. 'What do you suggest we order?' Sam asked.

After a short discussion, the man went away again and I asked Sam, 'What occasion are we celebrating with such a fine wine?' The meal was obviously going to cost more than one at my local *locanta*.

'We are celebrating that you are still alive,' Sam replied. 'And that I did not find your body in one of those awful drawers in the cold room.'

A waiter soon appeared with an array of appetizers: stuffed vine leaves, which were always a favourite, a beetroot salad with yoghurt, and *sigara böreği* – crispy cheese pastries. This was followed by baked savoury noodles filled with minced meat known as *manti*. I could barely eat it all but I did save room for a rose-flavoured dessert known as *su muhallebisi*. This one was particularly delicious as it was lightly flavoured with mastica and cardamom. In fact it was so delicious one would never have known there was food rationing in Turkey.

Throughout the meal we spoke about our lives back in England and America. Sam said he had a wife who was living with her parents in South Carolina while he was away. He missed her very much. He asked about my marriage and I told him that I too missed Dorothy. At the thought of her, I felt a pang of guilt, yet it was not enough to make me want to give up Ilona. I even wondered if she might be having an affair too.

'In a way, you and I are similar,' he said. 'We miss our wives yet take comfort in the arms of another woman.' There was a pause. 'I wonder if we can ever go back to civilian life unchanged. Somehow I doubt it?'

We also talked about politics and whether the Turks would eventually stop being neutral. We both agreed that they would when they saw there was no hope for Germany.

'The Turks will side with the winners,' I replied, 'and it will be business as usual.'

Sam shook his head. 'Not quite. We – the Allies – still can't trust the Russians, even though they are on our side now and we need them. Stalin drives a hard bargain. The end of the war might very well morph into something else and I fear the aftermath could become messy.'

'As it did after the Great War.'

'Possibly even worse. We know that Hitler has been developing secret weapons that could wreak havoc on the world. Our spy networks have already kept us informed about that. With each war, the stakes get higher.'

The waiter came to clear the plates away and we were brought a Turkish coffee and cubes of lokum on the house. They certainly were looking after us. Out of the window, I watched the seagulls hovering near a small brightly coloured fishing vessel as the men hauled their catch out of the boat to waiting restaurateurs. Their catch dispersed, the boat headed out to sea again. I had always loved being by the water and, for a brief time, I felt at peace, but it didn't last long.

'What I don't understand,' I said, reverting back to the murders, 'is what happened the first time I was supposed to meet the accountant – if it indeed it was him, which seems likely?'

'There seems to be only one conclusion to that as far as I can see,' Sam replied. 'The man knew he was being followed that time and must have confronted the person following him. A tussle occurred and the man was shot. The accountant would have known it was the Gestapo, which is why he took the ID. He was lucky that time, but his luck ran out.'

'Maybe he should just have walked away. The Gestapo would know if one of their own was murdered, and they certainly would have known he was on the trail of someone. Their tentacles are wide-reaching. For every dead Gestapo, there are half a dozen more. The accountant should have laid low for a while. He reached out again too soon and it was his undoing.'

'This makes us realise the information that the man was trying to pass was urgent. He really was a brave man,' I said. 'But how did he know about me? Why single me out and not you – or someone else in OSS?'

'Maybe he saw you with Ilona and put two and two together. He certainly would have known Messner liked her singing and would have seen her performing throughout the Reich. Who knows?'

Sam paid for the meal and we took a stroll back along the quayside. The air was fresh and the icy blasts of the past two weeks had passed over. I breathed in the fresh sea air, which did me the world of good, but I had the feeling that we'd come to a dead end.

'Cheer up, Elliot,' said Sam. 'This probably means that you won't be getting any more secret messages: no more lurking about in the shadows after midnight.' He laughed. 'Look at it this way – you've had a lucky escape.'

We parted ways and Sam took the tram back to Sultanahmet while I walked up the hill back to Galata. With Ilona at the Rose Noir, I had time to think. Her clothes filled the bedroom; a feather boa hung over the oval standing mirror and the dressing table was covered in jars of cream, brushes for her hair, a multitude of brushes for face powder, and an array of lipsticks and nail varnish. I couldn't bear the thought of her not being here. Trying not to get too depressed, I sat up until the early hours of the morning working at my typewriter on the kitchen table, attempting to write that novel I'd told Lady Celia, Kulin, and Banu about. It was a murder mystery – a love triangle – and I had no idea how it would end. How apt that it resembled my own life.

Ilona came home early and we made love as we used to, with a passion as if each time was the last. Afterwards we lay together making small talk. She told me about the customers and the songs she sang. Her eyes lit up when she talked about her work. It was her love. She pulled the sheet over us and I pulled it away.

'Don't cover yourself. I want to remember you just as you are now – Eve, the temptress – perfection.'

She laughed. 'Oh, Édesem drágám, don't be so melodramatic. I will be back before you know it.'

Over the next three nights, I tried to spend as much time in her company as possible. I went to the Rose Noir and watched her perform, I filled the apartment with flowers, and every night we made love. Then she was gone. Sam refused to let me see her off at Sirkeci Station in case we were being watched. He said both he and Macfarland would make sure she caught the train safely. The band had a lot of luggage and were travelling first class, so Macfarland paid someone handsomely to make sure Ilona's own luggage, especially the suitcase containing the money for Messner's Resistance group, was safely stored in her first class sleeping cabin.

It was ten days before Christmas and I drowned my sorrows in raki.

CHAPTER 9

It took a few days for me to get used to not having Ilona around. On orders from Sam, all her belongings were cleared out of my apartment and taken to her own near the Pera Palace. He said it was a precautionary measure just in case anyone was still watching me. In a matter of days, the smell I had become used to – her perfume, the scent of her body after lovemaking – faded, replaced by copious amounts of alcohol and tobacco. Sam did not hesitate to let me know that if I didn't snap out of my melancholy, he would take me off the job and I would be sent to Cairo and given a new assignment, most likely in Greece, where the Germans were still wreaking havoc, particularly after the Italians had surrendered.

For the Christians, Christmas celebrations were an excuse to let their hair down and escape from the monotony of politics, which were still mired in intrigues between all sides, including the Turks. There had been so many talks and conferences, yet no matter how hard we tried, we could not persuade the Turks to act in our favour. Rumour had it that Churchill was running out of patience trying to appease everyone. Naturally, the Germans were aware of all this, due in part we believed, and despite assurances to the contrary, that Turkish foreign minister Hüseyin Numan Menemencioğlu was pro-German. We were also convinced spies were reporting back to von Papen. Because of all this, Allied-Turkish relations were further strained.

My British and American friends tried to cheer me up by inviting me to lavish parties at their homes or get-togethers in some of Istanbul's most prestigious hotels. Occasionally I went to the Rose Noir, but the posters of the Budapest Gypsy Band featuring Ilona Lazlo made me feel even gloomier. Ilona's friend, Rozsika, tried to cheer me up too, offering at least twice, to spend the night with me – to "ease my comfort", as she put it. She was a chestnut-haired beauty who turned heads, but I politely declined, even though she promised not to breathe a word to Ilona. Even Boris was not his usual self. He had replaced Ilona and the band with another from Berlin – a swing band with a singer whose looks and voice reminded me of Zarah Leander, the Swedish actress and singer the Nazis had fallen in love with. She had the same confident style, with a deep contralto voice.

Boris came and joined me one evening and handed me a fine Cuban cigar. 'What do you think of them?' he asked. 'The singer certainly has sex appeal, wouldn't you agree?'

'Not my style,' I answered.

He laughed, knowing that I was smitten with Ilona. 'I hired them on cheaper rates due to public and private dance events in the Reich officially being prohibited after the defeat at Stalingrad. That madman, Goebbels, proclaiming 'total war' early this year has signalled the end for most of the dance venues. Where will they play?' he asked, shaking his head. 'Those fortunate enough to flee have come to cities like Istanbul. They count themselves lucky to simply play for a cheap room and a good meal. The other option was to stay, which would have meant the men would most likely be sent to the Eastern Front. I wouldn't wish that on my worst enemy.'

I asked about Ilona. Had he heard from her?

'No, but don't worry, she will be fine. She *is* Hungarian, and after all – as we all know – there are rules for the top brass, and rules for everyone else. Life for those in the Nazi hierarchy will go on as normal. They will drink champagne and fine wines, eat the best food, and listen to good music. So you see, my dear man, Ilona will be guaranteed work.'

I often wondered if Boris realised she was doing clandestine work. If he did, he kept quiet about it. It wasn't often he talked about politics, and I was interested in his thoughts. 'But Hungary is siding with the

Nazis,' I said. 'They've sent troops to fight the Soviets.'

He shrugged. 'That's true, but it is my opinion, for what it's worth, that Horthy, while sharing some of Hitler's views, especially when it comes to Communism, still believes in a Western victory. I think he continues to help them in order to have some semblance of self-rule, regardless of how limited. We must also remember that whilst many Hungarian Jews have not had life easy, especially in the countryside, not all have yet been deported. This will certainly be in his favour should the Allies win.' He twirled the cigar between his manicured hands, showing off his ostentatious, bejewelled rings. 'I despise this game of politics. Business suits me better and right now, business is not as brisk without Ilona.'

I asked him what he thought of the current situation vis-à-vis the Turks still maintaining neutrality, to which he replied that he thought the Turks were wise. 'They know how to play the game. Don't worry,' he said with the air of a Russian who had seen what revolutions can do to people, 'they will eventually side with the Allies. The problem is Stalin. If the Allies can keep him at bay, İnönü will like that. The last thing they want is the Russians storming the Caucasus.'

By now I knew enough of Turkish history to wholeheartedly agree.

On Christmas Day, Sir Richard and Lady Celia invited me to dinner, which, to my surprise was not the intimate affair I'd expected, but instead, a gathering of important British and Americans. Ambassador Knatchbull-Hugessen was there, as were Macfarland and Sam, along with Harold Gibson, head of MI6 in Istanbul. Sam was in a particularly good mood because Claudine was in Istanbul for the week and she had also been invited. It was at this dinner that I was introduced to a raven-haired woman called Leila. I was seated between her and someone who worked for the BBC Turkish Service who I'd met on a previous occasion and who knew Turkish and Turkey extremely well. We were aware the BBC had a growing following from Turkish people, which is why he was closely monitored by the ambassador, who did his best not to upset the Turks in any way. This man was an easy-going chap with a quick wit, and Lady Celia was particularly fond of him, so much so that I could never quite tell if it was merely the sociable side of her doing her duty for her husband and country, or something else.

The day was a convivial affair as always. Lady Celia had an excellent Turkish cook. Much to everyone's delight, the esteemed cook, always eager to please, had now become an expert on mince pies and Christmas puddings too. After the meal, Sir Richard invited him into the room and a speech was made in honour of his fine food. With a serious face, he thanked everyone, took a polite bow, and quickly exited the room, obviously embarrassed to receive such an accolade.

Throughout the meal, Leila and I made small talk. She asked me how long I had been in Istanbul and what I did for a living. I told her I was a newspaper correspondent and was in the process of writing a fiction book. We talked a lot about writers – she liked Hemingway, who she had met once – Steinbeck, and the Russian writers. We even talked about carpets as she said she had just purchased a fine one from a carpet dealer near the Grand Bazaar. She asked if I was going to purchase one to send home while I had the chance. It was all very easy-going. She had a beautiful English accent, one that reminded me of Dorothy, and told me she had studied there for a few years as an archaeologist. Her mother was an English countess and her father an Egyptian archaeologist who spent much of his time in the Valley of the Kings. She laughed. 'He wants to be like Howard Carter and discover an unopened tomb in all its splendour, so we very rarely see him. Mother is most patient.'

She seemed a warm person with a quiet confidence, and I found her delightful company. After dinner, we all retired to the drawing room and talked about the latest news. We had just received word that US General Dwight D. Eisenhower had become the Supreme Allied Commander in Europe. The war in the Pacific was still raging, but with this news, we were well and truly going to give the Nazis something to worry about. We all agreed that it was impossible to fight Britain, the United States, *and* Russia. The Germans didn't have the resources or the manpower, which was mostly slave labour and subject to sabotage. Our spirits boosted, we listened to Bing Crosby singing "White Christmas" whilst drinking port or bandy and roasting chestnuts on the blazing fire, which made most of us nostalgic. Very soon, we were dancing to Benny Goodman and Glenn Miller. It was certainly an optimistic Christmas.

At one point, I found myself alone with Macfarland. 'How are you, Elliot? Any more secret messages?' He laughed when I told him no, or I should say it was more of a smirk, as if it was all a joke even though two people had been shot and there were red flags everywhere. Sam saw us and must have noticed how uncomfortable I looked as he left his mistress and came over to join us.

'I've been meaning to catch up with you,' he said, 'but with Christmas, I've had a lot on my plate.' He glanced at the redhead and I understood exactly what he meant.

Macfarland excused himself and went over to talk with Harold Gibson. 'He dislikes me,' I said, after he'd gone. 'He thinks I'm paranoid.'

Sam put his hand on my shoulder. 'He likes to think he has everything under control, that's all. Don't take it personally.'

'Have you any more news about the network?'

'Our sources in Cairo have just received vital information that Field Marshal Wilhelm Keitel has ordered that V-1 rockets attack London in a few weeks' time. Although there appears to be no V-1s yet in production, it is imperative we destroy their production facilities. I believe Ilona will be meeting up with an Austrian, possibly Messner himself, shortly after Christmas. Everything is on track to get at least one wireless transmitter and receiver here by the time she gets back. When that happens we will be able to parachute in one of our experienced radiomen to liaise with the resistants more effectively. For the moment, Messner and Issakides are at home celebrating Christmas with their families. One thing seems certain though, if the accountant was trying to warn us of something, it appears to have stopped with his death, and we have no more reason to be worried. All is going smoothly.' He changed the subject. 'How did you find Miss Leila? Charming, isn't she?'

I looked at him and raised an eyebrow. 'What are you up to now?'

He gave me one of his cheeky grins. 'I'm giving you a few weeks off. Call it a well-earned holiday, although I can't exactly say you'll be putting your feet up.' He leaned closer. 'Macfarland had a meeting with SOE and in the interests of friendly relations, it seems that OSS is willing to let you go back to helping the British for a few weeks.' This was not what I'd expected to hear. 'Well, don't look like a stunned mullet or people will think something's wrong. You could at least smile. I'd have thought you'd appreciate a holiday.'

'Is this some kind of joke?'

'Certainly not! Do I look like I'm joking?' He took a puff on his cigar.

'Are you sending me away because of what's happened? Am I going to Cairo – or elsewhere?'

'Nothing like that. The British would like you to do something for them. I think we can spare you for a couple of weeks.'

Then it dawned on me. I'd purposely been placed next to Leila for that reason. When I asked if she had anything to do with it, Sam said yes, but he would leave it to someone at SOE to tell me. 'Don't worry. This has all been sanctioned from higher up – London and Cairo – but for security issues, we don't want the British Intelligence Service involved, and especially not the ambassador. Do you understand?'

'Of course.'

'Good. Go and pay them a visit tomorrow morning. You know where their offices are. I know it's Christmas, but in Turkey, this is not a holiday and it's business as usual.' Claudine came over to join us and looped her arm through his affectionately, hinting that he'd left her alone for too long.

'Alright, my dear,' Sam said. 'I'm coming.' He quickly whispered in my ear. 'Be at their office tomorrow at ten o'clock sharp. And by the way, we will maintain your apartment while you're gone: pick up the mail and that sort of thing, make it look as though it's occupied. You know what I mean.'

I knew he exactly what he meant. Would there be any letters from Ilona, which was highly improbable, or more importantly, would there be any more secret letters? I looked across the room and saw Leila chatting with Gibson and Lady Celia. She gave me a quick look, nodded, and smiled. She had known about this all along and not uttered a word. Small talk indeed: she was a cool character and had been testing me out.

The next day I arrived at the offices of the Goeland Shipping Company, where SOE operated from. Due to Christmas, I was surprised to find it still busy. A pool of secretaries was busily typing away amidst desks filled with folders. I went to the nearest one and introduced myself. She appeared to be expecting me.

'Good morning, Mr Caldwell,' she said, adjusting her rather oversized spectacles to peer at me over the typewriter. 'Mr Mackintosh is expecting you – room eight.' She indicated a set of double doors leading to a stuffy corridor with beautifully framed etchings of steam ships along the wall. I knocked on the door and a voice called out, 'Come in.' Inside, standing by the window with his hands clasped behind his back, was head of SOE Turkey, Lieutenant Colonel John Ali (Jack) Mackintosh.

He turned to face me and shook hands. 'Hello, George, or should I call you Elliot now? It's been quite a while since I last saw you. How are you?'

'Fine, thank you.'

'Take a seat. Make yourself comfortable. Would you like a cup of tea or that dreadful thick stuff that passes for coffee here?' I rather liked Turkish coffee but said I would join him a cup of tea. 'I trust our friend the ambassador is not aware of your presence here. He seems to think our activities might upset the status quo.'

'No, sir. I am aware of his attitude.'

'Well, I must say, I'm glad to have you back with us, even though it's only for a few weeks.'

A secretary brought in tea and shortbread biscuits. I couldn't resist smiling at the sight of the shortbread biscuits. It was all very British. Mackintosh asked why I was smiling.

'For a man who's spent a lot of time in the Balkans and the Middle East, I would have thought you would have acquired a taste for Turkish food. After all, it's very good.'

'I agree wholeheartedly, and I have eaten enough sugar-laced sweets in my time to rot my teeth, but these biscuits were a Christmas gift from Lady Celia. That cook of hers excels at them.'

'Yes. I had one of his mince pies last night.'

'Now, down to business.'

'Where are you sending me,' I asked. 'When do I fly out?'

Mackintosh burst out laughing. 'Oh no; it's nothing of the sort. You're not flying anywhere. This assignment is internal – here in Turkey – but not in Istanbul.'

On the wall behind him was a large map of Turkey showing countries surrounding the Black Sea, the Aegean, and the Mediterranean. The major ports were all marked with a circle. Next to it was a smaller map of Turkey and her Middle Eastern neighbours. He picked up a long stick, swung his chair around, and pointed to a few places on the coast opposite the Greek Islands. He reminded me of my old geography teacher except that he wasn't pointing out Niagara Falls or the Amazon. The tip of the stick stopped on the first place – Kuşadası, and then moved to another –Fethiye.

'So I am to help the Greek resistance?' It was more of a statement than a question.

'Spot on.'

That didn't sound too difficult. It was common knowledge that many Greeks and Allied soldiers had fled the Nazi occupation there and passed through Turkey, albeit clandestinely.

'You will be taking a few Greeks to safety. They will be heading to Cyprus rather than trying to get through Syria. The British have stopped accepting Jews in Palestine.'

'Greek Jews?'

'Most of them. The two of you will have to decide on the best route depending on the circumstances.' He moved his stick across the map. 'Antalya is your destination.'

'The two of us?'

Mackintosh put down his stick. 'Yes, didn't Sam tell you? Leila will be joining you. She knows the area well.'

'I'd already gathered I was seated next to her at Lady Celia's for a reason.'

He laughed again. 'And you passed with flying colours. Leila is a good judge of character and if she'd taken a dislike to you, you wouldn't be here right now.' He went on to explain the assignment more. 'From Antalya, you will take the escapees to waiting boats and once they are out of Turkish waters, that part of your work is done. The next part is probably the most difficult. At the same time, you will be given a cache of arms which you will drop off here.' He picked the stick up again and pointed to a place near Fethiye.

'So I will be gun-running. You know what will happen if we're caught. There'll be a diplomatic issue.'

Mackintosh's face turned deadly serious. 'Then for your sake, you'd better not get caught. You know how it works. We will deny all knowledge of you and you will most likely be shot. So don't get caught because I promised Sam you would get back here safe and sound.'

That was usually how these missions started: a charming smile over a cup of tea, and in this case, shortbread biscuits – as if we were in a Lyons Tea House in London– and the denial of everything if someone was caught. It always made me wonder why so many were prepared to put their life on the line: freedom with a huge dose of idealism and notions of romantic values. How many unclaimed bodies littered the earth in the pursuit of this elusive thing called freedom and democracy? Thousands, I imagined, and I certainly didn't want to be one of them.

'Now that's all settled,' Mackintosh said, 'I want you to dine alone at the Park Hotel. The bill is on us. Someone will bring you an envelope containing an address in the Princes Islands –Büyükada. From there you will continue by boat to Yalova with your new identity papers, which you will use once you get out of the straits. Deposit your existing papers with this man in Büyükada and pick them up on the way back.' He sat back in the chair and asked if I had any questions.

'What will be my excuse for travelling?'

'You will be working as a carpet exporter for the Oriental Trading Company, a fictitious company set up by us, but with contacts used by both OSS and ourselves. I think you know who I mean.'

'Just to be clear, are we talking about Mustafa from Galeri Pandora?'

Jack smiled. 'We are: a trustworthy man with extensive contacts.'

'So that's why Leila was asking me about carpets?'

'Of course! You should know by now, there is no such thing as small talk here. It always leads somewhere.'

'Where will I meet Leila?'

'At the Grand Hotel in İzmir. She will be expecting you. From there you will be travelling together.' He paused for a moment. 'There is one more thing. I know you speak Turkish and I note from your files that you are fluent in Greek, but please don't attempt to converse in Greek if you can help it, not even to the escapees or the resistance. Only English. I don't have to tell you why. It could raise suspicions with the Turks, but I do want you to use your language skills to listen in to their conversations. If you pick up anything that could be relevant to us, no matter how small, you can reach me here.' He gave me the telephone number and asked me to memorize it before destroying it.

I left the building with a strange feeling. On the one hand, I was going to the place of my birth, but on the other hand, I was to maintain my Englishness and I felt confused emotions. It was also highly dangerous, but at least it would distract me from worrying about Ilona and whether I would get any more secret messages.

CHAPTER 10

AT THE PARK Hotel, a small table had already been booked for me and I ordered a whisky on the rocks while casting my eyes around the room to see if I recognized anyone. The only person I knew was Mathilde, who was with a German officer. Our eyes met but she diplomatically pretended not to know me. It occurred to me that she too might be an agent, gathering information on someone's behalf, and I hoped it wasn't about me. But from what Ilona had told me, I doubted she was a German agent. She was a shrewd woman and did what she could to survive, using the Germans to her advantage. The waiter brought over the whisky and deposited a large red leather-bound menu in front of me.

'I will give you a few minutes and come back to take your order,' he said. 'The dish of the day is chicken in a spicy orange sauce.'

I always enjoyed dining at the Park. The food was excellent. They served a combination of classic Ottoman dishes and European favourites, guaranteed to please everyone. They certainly had established a good clientele, including Sir Richard and Lady Celia, but it was also a favourite of the Germans. The atmosphere was excellent too, being somewhat more intimate than the Pera Palace. My table was set against the wall, which was covered in mirrors, between which were placed small lamps, casting a warm glow on the surrounding tables. It occurred to me that I'd never brought Ilona here and I vowed to do it when she returned. In the corner was a pianist who had an extensive repertoire of romantic music. Occasionally, he was joined by a violinist who would serenade the couples at their request. The Germans and Austrians particularly enjoyed this as it reminded them of restaurants at home.

An hour later, after I had feasted on meze and salads, and the delicious chicken in spicy orange sauce, accompanied by an excellent white wine, there was still no sign of an envelope. Every time someone entered the room, I wondered if they would head over to me. My table was cleared and the waiter brought the dessert menu and asked if I would like to order. He stood there while I opened it. Inside was a manila envelope. He had deliberately positioned himself where I could slip it into my jacket without anyone noticing. Finally!

The waiter continued describing the dessert as if all was quite normal. 'We have a choice of cakes and tarts.' He indicated towards another waiter, who was cutting a slice of meringue from the cake trolley for a customer. 'Or we have our chef's favourites.'

I decided on the *peynir tatlisi* – the cheese sponges in syrup, even though I was quite full. I could never resist Turkish sweets.

After this, I left and headed home to check the contents of the envelope. There was a new passport in the name of Jerome Burchett, carpet exporter for the Oriental Trading Company. With it was a travel pass and tickets that would take me all the way to İzmir. With everything in order, I packed my bag and left the apartment early in the morning to catch the ferry to Büyükada.

A thick fog had settled over the Bosphorus and for a while we weren't sure if the boat would travel, but after a delay of only half an hour, we were on our way. I recalled one of the old writers saying that the skyline of Istanbul – with its mosques and minarets, its Byzantine walls interspersed with gardens dotted with Cyrus trees – was better seen from the water. Unfortunately, this morning was not one of them. The wind had dropped and so had the temperature. Thankfully, heading south, I would miss the snow. After a quick breakfast of hot tea and a slice of pie from the vendors who sold their wares on the boat, I settled down to reading a book and arrived in Büyükada just over an hour later.

Already the small jetty was packed with more vendors hoping to do a brisk trade from the first boat of the day. I made my way to a white house surrounded by a walled garden just off the main thoroughfare. There, I was met by an Englishman, handed him my original IDs, and stayed for a few hours with him until the ferry left for Yalova. The man had an Italian father and, as he spoke fluent Italian, had been posted to Italy until his network was betrayed by someone in the Italian resistance who was caught a few months later and talked under torture. He managed to escape to Malta and then to Cairo. SOE Cairo sent him to work in Istanbul, and Mackintosh allowed him to operate from the island as a sort of intermediary for people like myself, coming from and going to Istanbul. He was also one of SOE's few radiomen in the country, which meant he had access to the latest news. It was here that I learned of a tragedy in Italy in the Italian port of Bari. Many were killed and another 545 were injured after a surprise air raid by eighty-eight Luftwaffe bombers. Unbeknownst to anyone except its commanding officers, an American merchant marine ship had been carrying a cargo of two thousand mustard gas bombs. The ship was one of seventeen Allied vessels that were sunk in the raid, but managed to stay afloat until its deadly cargo exploded. He also told me that the first Jews were being shipped out of Italy. A few weeks earlier, on December 6, a train took prisoners from Milan and Verona to the Auschwitz concentration camp.

He wished me a safe trip and I caught the ferry to Yalova. Our conversation cast a dark cloud over me. What was happening to the Jews of Italy would certainly be happening to the Jews of Greece.

My journey to İzmir was comfortable and without any problems. Twice I was asked for my papers, questioned, and let go as they were perfect forgeries. The fact that I spoke Turkish also endeared me to the people in the same carriage, especially on the last leg to İzmir. Most of them were rural Turks and hoped the war would end soon as rationing was affecting their lives and livelihood. Nearing İzmir, I took the opportunity to have a smoke alone in the corridor. I pulled down the window and breathed in the air of Anatolia, trying to picture the land of my forebears before the collapse of the Ottoman Empire. The train passed through miles and miles of olive groves with their gnarled trunks and shimmering grey-green leaves. Occasionally the train stopped at a small town with stone and timber houses, a couple of mosques with spindly minarets, and what looked like the ruins of what would once have been a fine house – possibly Greek. I felt a sudden anger at my father for hiding my background from me for so long, but that quickly subsided when I thought how much easier it was for him to try and forget the past. As for my stepmother, I'd never liked her but now I hated her even more. Why had she made my father hide his past, and especially his first marriage?

It was late afternoon when the train pulled into İzmir station, and I headed to the Grand Hotel. A room had already been booked in my name – Jerome Burchett. The receptionist handed the key to a porter who carried my one suitcase to my room, opened the curtains and the French doors leading to a small terrace just big enough to hold a small table and two chairs, and told me if I needed anything to call reception. I tipped him and he left.

I stepped out onto the terrace and looked at the esplanade. The sun was setting, casting a warm red glow on the water. Even though it was winter, people were still promenading, albeit in warm winter clothes rather than in summer clothes and with parasols as I had seen in photographs of the city before it lay in ruins after the great fire which destroyed most of it in September 1922. Even that had been kept from me until my conversation with my father. The city had certainly changed over those years.

I wondered if I should take a walk to discover just how much of my parents' world still existed, but decided against it. I wasn't here to wallow in self-pity and a life I never knew. The telephone on the bedside table rang.

It was Leila. 'Welcome to İzmir, Jerome. Are you going to join me in the Atatürk Bar for a drink?'

I changed into a decent suit and made my way downstairs. She was sitting at the bar drinking a martini and gracefully smoking a cigarette in a long black cigarette holder. She was dressed in a simple, yet stunning azure dress of watered silk and looked as beautiful as ever. The neckline was wide and low, almost off the shoulder, and she wore a gold necklace and matching bracelet. She wore her dark hair to one side, allowing it to tumble over one shoulder in long tresses. I gave her a peck on the cheek as if we were close friends.

'What will you have?' she asked.

'Whisky on the rocks.'

'I presume you had no problems getting here?'

'Not at all. In fact, it makes a change to get out of Istanbul. When did you arrive?'

'Yesterday. All is ready for our journey. How do you feel about it?'

'I've been put at your disposal. I'm presuming you've done this before?'

She put the tip of her ebony cigarette holder between her lips and inhaled. 'Quite a few times, but it never gets any easier. We always have to be careful.'

After our drink, she suggested a fish restaurant along the quayside. 'The food here is excellent, but the other is one of the best restaurants in town, and they play the best music.'

I held her coat while she slipped into it. Her perfume reminded me of Ilona. The restaurant was at the far end of the promenade and was packed. We were lucky to find a table as the group who were playing were apparently famous. They played the old-style Smyrniot music, which I found intensely moving. There was a small orchestra in the centre of the room consisting of about eight to ten musicians and two singers. The instruments were a violin, the traditional qanun, oud and tambours, and a ney. I had been to cafes in Istanbul and heard some of this music, but this group was particularly accomplished.

'I believe you speak Turkish well,' Leila said. 'In which case you will understand what they are singing about.'

I had to admit to myself that my Turkish did not stretch to understanding the songs as I would have liked, but more than that, I found it emotional. Had my parents listened to such music? I certainly never heard any in the house I grew up in. Leila picked up on how much the music moved me. She laughed and in Turkish said that I had the soul of a Turk. I did not comment. It was an enjoyable evening with excellent food, particularly the İzmir köfte, which I was informed, was one of the city's best dishes.

We retired to our rooms early that evening. 'Get a good night's sleep,' Leila said. 'Tomorrow after breakfast, we leave for Kuşadası.'

I didn't go straight to bed. Instead, I sat on the veranda watching the silvery moon slip into the water on the horizon, wondering what might have happened if my parents hadn't left Turkey. Was it fate that brought me back here? My father was a superstitious man and I think he would have known in his heart that one day, I would be back here. Unfortunately he would never have imagined under what circumstances, and now it was too late to tell him. He died before the outbreak of the war.

We left İzmir straight after breakfast in an old tarpaulin-covered truck partially filled with rolls of handmade carpets conveniently supplied by Mustafa's connections from his warehouse in the city. Leila and I decided to take the driving in turns as the journey, although not far, was bumpy and hazardous and we needed to keep our wits about us. She had shed her beautiful azure dress and was wearing wide dark brown cotton trousers with a simple white shirt and a thick pullover.

'I'll drive first,' she said. 'You can make yourself useful by reading the map to make sure we don't get lost. It's easily done.'

The truck rumbled out of the city, heading for Kuşadası, which wasn't a long drive. We were stopped twice and our papers and the contents of the truck were checked. At Kuşadası, we stopped for a snack and swapped places. Our first stop was a small seaside village opposite Samos where there was a small inn with an owner who turned a blind eye to helping the Greeks for a small sum of money. Here we would spend the night while we waited for word from our contact. Sometime after midnight, Leila knocked on my door and told me our first package had arrived. We quietly made our way outside to where we'd parked the truck, next to an olive grove and away from the main road. Two Turks were there with a man called Stavros, who Leila said belonged to the Greek resistance. We shook hands and he thanked me for what I was doing. I longed to tell him I was one of them but resisted the urge.

Stavros regularly crossed between Samos and the Turkish mainland bartering goods before the war broke out, and he was used to the area. He knew every village and cove between there and Rhodes, and since the German and Italian occupation, had set up small networks along the coast. 'How many?' Leila asked, referring to the escapees.

'A family of four. Jews from Salonika: the parents and two teenage girls. The parents are stoic and the children terrified.'

'Where are they?'

One of the men went back into the olive grove and brought them out. The two girls cowered behind their parents. 'It's alright,' Leila said in Turkish, stroking the smallest girl's head gently. She told Stavros to assure them they were safe.

'Where will we hide?' the man said.

Leila pointed to the truck. 'It won't be the most comfortable of rides, but no one will search there.'

The men pulled down the back of the truck and jumped on top of the carpets, pushing some aside so that they could get on board. The family worked their way to the back, where a space had been made for them. In fact, the truck might have looked as if it was filled with carpets but the back half was empty. Being winter, it was still cold and blankets had been supplied for them.

'Tell them we'll bring them food in the morning but they must keep very quiet,' Leila added.

Stavros did as she asked and I was pleased that I understood his words. They were kind and showed great empathy for the family's plight. We pulled the tarpaulin back down and Leila gave several hundred lira to the Turks, who disappeared back into the olive grove while Stavros came inside to inform us of what was taking place in Greece. By the soft lamplight in Leila's room, he told us of the massacres in August at Kommeno, a village near Arta, and the massacre at Kalavryta in the Peloponnese which had occurred just a few weeks earlier. It was believed that the Germans had deported over 40,000 Jews from Salonika to Auschwitz-Birkenau so far. Stavros had tears in his eyes when he told us he'd heard that the SS murdered virtually all of the Salonika Jews upon arrival.

'The Allies may have gained some ground but the Germans are digging in and it's only a matter of time before the Jews of Athens are deported too. Add to that they have tightened reconnaissance of fishing vessels they think are carrying refugees. We've already lost several men.'

After delivering more depressing news from Greece, Stavros left and we tried to get a few hours' sleep before starting out again the next morning. Leila managed to procure bread, olives, and cheese for the Jewish family. After the starvation that had seen hundreds of thousands die in their homeland, they were grateful for anything. We continued on to Fethiye and Patara, where it was particularly dangerous because of the German base in Rhodes, and did the same thing. Near Fethiye we picked up another group: two young women in their twenties and a middle-aged man. Near Patara we collected three women and a six-year-old boy who had just managed to evade a German patrol boat. The truck was now full, with the escapes crammed together behind the carpets.

From Patara, we headed back and then across land to Kızıldağ, a beautiful mountainous area in the Yenişarbademli-Şarkikaraağaç-Aksu districts of Isparta Province. The air was fresh and the forests filled with glorious cedar trees. Travelling along this route meant we hardly encountered any traffic or army vehicles and were able to stop in the occasional village to stock up on food for us all. The road was winding and tough in places, which slowed us down, but Leila assured us we were still on schedule. When it was safe, we stopped and allowed the escapees to stretch their legs and get some fresh air, but it was never longer than thirty minutes, then we were off again. At night we hid them in a cave or an abandoned house while we slept in one of the few small hotels which doubled up as a shop and garage for the people in the area. At dawn we set off again, making sure we had enough food for the rest of the group. The owners were only too happy to get some money as trade was hardly brisk. In two days we reached our destination – Antalya. About fifteen kilometres outside of the city, Leila told me to take a sharp turn and head for a rocky cove. The road took us over scrubland and was extremely bumpy, and I was afraid we would burst a tyre. After a mile or two, the road started to veer downwards and I got my first glimpse of the sea.

'Keep going,' Leila said. 'We're nearly there.'

Eventually we reached a small wooded area that led down to a cove. Three men were waiting at the bottom, waving. 'We made it,' she said. 'You did well.'

When we reached the cove, the men surrounded the truck and helped move the carpets away in order for the escapees to get out. They looked as relieved as I was.

An elderly Turkish man called Orhan came to greet us. He shook my hand vigorously. 'How was the trip? Any problems?'

'None at all,' Leila replied. She introduced me as Jerome, another carpet dealer from İzmir. Orhan laughed and commented on how many carpet dealers there were these days.

The group of Jews piled out of the truck, with the children running towards the water. 'Come back,' one of the women shouted.

'It's alright,' Leila said. 'They are safe here. This cove is protected and no one will see them. Let them have a moment of joy.'

We left our package there that night and went to find a comfortable hotel in Antalya. Leila made a call to someone and I overheard her say the carpets had arrived safe and sound.

'Do you want to go out for a meal?' she asked. 'Tomorrow we have a busy day. We take the carpets to the warehouse.'

I was too tired to eat and told her I just wanted to sleep. 'You did well, Jerome. Thank you.'

'Thank me when it's all over and we're back in İzmir.'

She laughed. 'I've made this trip several times and there's always tension. One never knows if the authorities will catch us, so I understand.' She gave me a peck on the cheek and bid me goodnight.

I woke in the morning to the call of the muezzin. It was a sound I'd come to love. I went down to the breakfast room, where Leila was seated at a table with four people. When she saw me enter the room, she waved me over. 'Jerome, come and meet my friends.'

All turned to look at me and when I saw one of them, I felt a lump rise in my throat. It was Füsun. What's more, she was pregnant. By the look on her face, she was as shocked to see me as I was to see her. I was introduced as Jerome Burchett. Everyone welcomed me heartily.

'Merhaba, Burchett Bey,' Füsun said, averting her eyes slightly.

It didn't go unnoticed by Leila. 'Do you two know each other?' she asked.

'I met him a couple of times with my father,' Füsun said, 'but we never spoke.'

The rest of the group were introduced, including Füsun's husband, who looked even fatter and uglier than his photograph. They were all in the carpet trade and sympathetic to our cause. After breakfast, we were taken to their warehouse, where several men were busily organising bales of carpets to be shipped overseas. Our carpets were taken from the truck and exchanged for bales of wool, all of which would be dyed back in İzmir. I found myself alone with Füsun for a few minutes and asked how she was.

'I'm fine. My husband is a good man so I cannot complain.' She rubbed her belly. 'We hope for a strong boy. Please give my love to my father.'

I told her I was pleased to see her, but I could tell she was no longer the woman I knew. The sparkle in her eyes had gone and she seemed to be losing her youth very fast. I felt sorry for her. Her lot was the lot of many Turkish women, despite Atatürk's reforms to lift women out of the old ways. Unlike other women I had met in Istanbul, she would live to serve her husband and her family. That was her priority now. I wished with all my heart that she could have met a nice foreigner – one of the OSS or SOE men that I knew who weren't married – but would that have made her happy? Probably not. Destiny was a constant part of Turkish culture and this was her destiny.

With the truck laden with bales of wool, we said our goodbyes and went back to the hotel. We paid for another night's room but left soon after dinner, heading back to the bay. Under cover of darkness, we joined the group and waited for two boats to arrive. They were on time. As they pulled into the shallows, the men waded in to collect boxes of guns and ammunition. Carefully, they piled the boxes onto the sand and after checking each one and a short discussion in Turkish, told us everything was in order. A bag of money was given to the men, and the Greek escapees were helped into the two boats.

This was a dangerous moment as they had to get out of Turkish waters without being spotted by the coastguards and patrol ships. We said our goodbyes, wishing them the best of luck, and watched the boats until they disappeared into the darkness of the night. After that, we loaded the boxes into the truck, hiding them as we had the Jews. When we were satisfied the bales were all secured back in place, Leila gave the men several thousand lira and we set off back to İzmir, taking the same route as we came.

This time, Leila was driving. 'It all went well,' she said. 'Within a few hours they should be in Cyprus. I am especially pleased that we received the weapons. There was more than I expected and SOE in Cairo have already told us they have more supplies ready. Some will be parachuted into Greece itself. They are certainly helping but it's always a gamble making sure they don't get into the wrong hands. However, we must be thankful for everything we get as this means a great deal to the Greek resistance.'

I asked her how well she knew Füsun and her husband.

'I first met Füsun at their warehouse in Istanbul. I barely know her. I didn't even know she'd gotten married until a few weeks ago. Why do you ask?'

'No reason. I just didn't expect to see her, that's all.'

'Did you know her well?'

'No. She was always there when we were in Mustafa's han. She struck me as being an innocent girl – most unworldly.'

Leila laughed. 'Don't underestimate Turkish women – or Middle Eastern women in general. They may not all have had the sort of upbringing I've had, but they are quite worldly in their own way. They know how to survive in what is still a patriarchal world. I must say though, I did find her husband an odd match for her. I would have though her father would have at least found a younger, better-looking man. The family is very well-known in the rug business, and they are wealthy. Perhaps he thought she would have a comfortable life.' She looked across at me. 'I can see you don't really understand the culture here, Jerome, despite having been here for a while. Not everyone is as free and as outgoing as Banu and her friends.'

Maybe she was right. I didn't understand them, especially the women.

After driving through the night, we stopped for a while in a village to have a meal, before carrying on again and staying in a hotel before the last part of the mission – giving the weapons to the Greek resistance. The next evening we finally ended up at the small seaside village opposite Samos. Leila went inside the same inn we had stayed at on our way through and the inn owner gave her directions to a secluded cove further on. After another bumpy ride, we arrived. But this time there was no waiting reception. Leila looked worried.

'Where's Stavros?' she asked, nervously. 'And the others – the Turks?'

'Maybe we should leave and park the truck elsewhere. We can always come back here on foot and hide.'

She agreed, so we hid the truck about a kilometre away, took our guns, and walked back to the cove, making sure we were well-hidden. 'It's not like them,' Leila said. 'Something must be wrong.'

We waited for over six hours. Finally, at three in the morning, a blue fishing boat came out of the darkness and landed in the shallows. Through her binoculars, Leila saw it was Stavros. 'Thank God, but where are the others?' We waited a few minutes and another boat appeared around the rocks. This time we went to join them.

'Sorry about the delay,' Stavros said. 'There have been too many patrol boats. The Germans have caught some smugglers and are extending their searches. We had to take refuge in another cove nearby.' With barely a pause, he asked if we had the weapons.

'Yes, but we have to go and get the truck. It wasn't safe to keep it here.'

'Hurry, we haven't much time. It will soon be dawn.'

I told Leila to stay with them while I went back to fetch the truck myself. As soon as I arrived, they started to unload the weapons. Stavros looked pleased. 'Bravo. Good work.'

When the boxes were loaded on to the boats, he shook my hand. 'Thank you. You are a good man.'

And then Leila turned to me. 'Goodbye, Jerome. This is where you and I part company. I'm honoured to have met you.'

I couldn't believe what I was hearing. 'Are you going too? What about getting back to İzmir? We haven't finished our mission.'

'This part of the mission is over for me. I am going to Greece with Stavros. SOE Cairo wants it that way. Wish me good luck.'

'Cairo be dammed,' I replied angrily. 'What if you get caught? What if *I* get caught?'

'Nothing will happen to you. You will go back to the hotel in İzmir and someone will be there waiting to take the truck from you. Your mission will then be finished. After that you go back to Istanbul and carry on as before.'

I was in too much shock to take it all in. She had never said a word about this. That made her a good agent, but I worried for her safety. Within five minutes, the boat was already starting to move away. Soon it disappeared from view, and I was left alone on the sandy beach. A sliver of silver moon peeked out from behind the clouds, and I was aware of the sea lapping against the rocks and the call of a bird from somewhere. I had never felt so alone in my life.

Back in İzmir, it was as she said; someone greeted me and took the truck with the bales of wool from me and the next day I left İzmir and my life as I had come to know it. This had been an interesting two weeks. More dangerous than I could have known, but I was glad to have had the opportunity to help. My father would have been proud of me.

CHAPTER 11

Istanbul was exactly as I had left it. Grey skies and cold weather, but at least it wasn't snowing. I got off the ferry with my old documents and headed straight back to the apartment. The door was unlocked. I took out my gun and slowly opened the door. The room smelt of sweet Turkish tobacco. A voice from the kitchen called out.

'Welcome home, Elliot.' It was Sam.

I threw down my hat on the sideboard and took off my coat. 'For heaven's sake. What are you doing here?'

'I came to check your mail.' He laughed. 'You're a day late.'

I was not in the mood to answer. Instead, I made myself a coffee.

'How did it go?' he asked.

'I think I should be debriefing to Jack Mackintosh, not you. After all, it wasn't an OSS mission.'

'Absolutely right, but I am glad to have you back safe and sound. Now it's back to business as usual. I have some good news. The first is that there have been no more secret messages, which means that they died with the murdered accountant, and the second is that Ilona will be back at the beginning of February. All went well with her work.'

This *was* good news. 'How long will she be here before she goes away again?'

'A month. We will receive the radio transmitter Messner asked for by then.'

Sam's smile faded. 'There is also some bad news, but that is for

Mackintosh to tell you.'

I felt a pounding in my chest and my throat went dry. 'What is it? If you know something, tell me now.'

He shook his head. 'No. This was an SOE mission. It is for him to do that.'

I put my hat and coat back on again and told him I was going to see Mackintosh straight away. Sam came with me as far as the Galata Bridge and we parted ways. 'I'll be having a drink in the bar at the Park if you feel like joining me,' he said.

When I arrived at SOE's offices at the Goeland Shipping Company, Mackintosh was waiting for me. He shook my hand and congratulated me on a good job. 'You will be pleased to know that the Jews arrived in Cyprus safe and sound.'

'I've just seen Sam. He told me there was bad news.'

He told me to take a seat. 'There's no good way of telling you this. Leila and Stavros were caught in Greek waters by a German patrol boat.'

I put my head in my hands. 'Leila and I suspected something was wrong but Stavros assured us they'd make it alright, even though there had been more night patrols. I was wary and recall leaving with a heavy heart. It was as if I knew something was going to happen.' My heart was thudding. I couldn't take it in. 'Do you know what's happened to them?'

'I am afraid that with the weapons on board, there was nothing they could say or do. I believe Stavros tried to kill himself, but the Germans stopped him. They were taken to Rhodes and interrogated. Both were then publicly hanged and were left in the square with a sign around their necks saying it was a warning to those who helped the resistance.' I felt the tears well up and bit my tongue to stop myself from crying. 'There's more bad news from Greece too. The Greek resistance has been causing havoc and the Germans have recruited more collaborators. Reprisals are taking place everywhere and, fearing an Allied landing, they have become involved in wide-ranging counter guerrilla operations, which they carry out with great efficiency, based on their experiences in Yugoslavia. Did Leila tell you about the massacres of Kommeno and Kalavryta?'

I nodded. 'Stavros told us. I also heard they burnt down the Monastery of Agia Lavra.'

Mackintosh shook his head. 'They knew that monastery was especially sacred to the Greeks because of its association with the Greek War of Independence. There are no words to describe it.' There was a silence between us while he allowed this news to sink in. He could tell how distressed I was. 'Leila was a good woman, Elliot, but she knew the risks. She may have died, but she's helped hundreds of refugees flee to safety and armed the resistance. We must be proud of her.' I was at a loss for anything to say. 'Thank you for what you did. We will carry on regardless. Others are willing to carry on the good fight in their place. It can't go on for much longer. The tide is turning.'

I walked out of his office in a daze. I couldn't take it in. Leila – hanged. It didn't seem real. That evening I drowned my sorrows with Sam in the bar at the Park.

'I know it wasn't good news,' Sam said. 'Try and look on the positive side. You got posted to Turkey, which is neutral.'

I threw him a dirty look. 'I wondered if that's what Messner's dead accountant thought, and the others who have ended up dead under suspicious circumstances.' He didn't reply.

I asked if he had any more news on the Maier-Messner group.

'I can tell you that their information on strategic armaments factories in Austria and Germany means that our bombing has been extremely accurate. Because of his contacts in the rubber and tyre industry, Messner has also shared with Dulles intelligence on Germany's formulation of synthetic rubber, a vital substance for the Reich since it had no sources for natural rubber. This includes the coordinates and production estimates for three rubber factories. It has enabled him to uncover plans to enhance German U-boats with sonar-resistant rubber panels. At this stage in the war, our destruction of vital infrastructure means that the Nazis cannot rebuild fast enough.'

'And their secret weapons?'

'Whenever we have information, they too are bombed. Dulles is very happy. The tide is turning.'

'You sound just like Mackintosh. He used those exact words.'

Sam switched from affability to seriousness, something that he could do in an instant. It was an art that he had mastered well. I often wondered who the real Sam was. 'For goodness sake, Elliot, look on the positive side – you are still alive.'

With those words ringing in my ears, I walked home, hoping the cold chill of an Istanbul winter would clear my head. He was right as usual: I had to snap out of it. The next few weeks were as normal. Snippets of information were passed from Cairo and Switzerland and we gathered information the best we could. In Europe, the Soviets were gaining ground and took Olevsk, not far from the pre-war Polish frontier, and the Reich Chancellery in Berlin was hit during an RAF raid. On one single night, British bombers conducted their heaviest raid on Berlin yet, dropping 2,300 tons of bombs in just over half an hour. We celebrated the success, yet still the Nazis dug in.

I often called by to see Lady Celia and Sir Richard. Lady Celia and her friends were constantly listening to the BBC. Being a true diplomat's wife, she never discussed anything she'd picked up through official sources, but she was often in a joyful mood, which spoke volumes.

And then, joy of joys, my heart soared when one evening I was invited to dinner at the Pera Palace and found Ilona there too, looking as ravishing as ever in a ruby red suit with a fox fur thrown over her shoulder, with her hair pulled back on one side and falling in soft waves over her shoulder. She carried herself with poise and style like one of those Russian princesses Boris used to entertain, who left Russia with their jewels and sparkled just as much until their money ran out. With her were Macfarland and Sam, and no matter how hard I tried, I could not conceal my joy. I was like a lovesick teenager. I gave her a peck on the cheek, inhaling her perfume, and told her I was glad she had arrived back safe and sound.

'How was the trip?' I asked.

Macfarland took over. 'That's what we were just discussing. Messner and an associate met her as planned in Budapest, but she found them nervous.'

'Is that true?' I asked. 'Did they say anything?'

'No, but I got the feeling they thought they were being watched,' Ilona said. 'I delivered them our "gift" for which they were very grateful, and they left, telling me to be careful. Nothing else.'

I looked at Sam and Macfarland's faces. You couldn't tell what they were thinking.

Macfarland was adamant all was fine in Istanbul and put it down to tightened security in the Reich. 'Everyone is being watched there,' he said. 'It's natural to be suspicious and on edge.'

'May I remind you, sir, that we are being watched here also.' I thought of the two murdered men. 'German intelligence is second to none.'

Macfarland's face reddened with anger. 'Watch your step, Elliot.'

Sam tried to cool things down. 'Ilona was never questioned and neither were any of the band. It is as we thought – who would question a well-known singer?' He turned to Ilona. 'Tell me, I presume Boris knows you're back.'

'Of course. We have star billing in a few days' time. You will come and see us, won't you?' she purred.

'Nothing would delight us more,' Sam said.

The evening was a mixture of emotions. I loathed Macfarland's company, as he did mine, but he knew Ilona and I were close so used it to his advantage, as did Sam. All I wanted was to take Ilona in my arms again. Despite patience being a prerequisite for a secret agent, I was not patient when it came to my feeling for Ilona. The evening drew to a close and, knowing that the three had things to talk about, I was the first to leave.

This time Ilona stood up and as she kissed me goodbye, her mouth brushed by my ear and she whispered softly, 'Goodnight, édesem.'

It was two days before I saw her again. She arrived at my apartment in the evening. I don't think I'd ever felt so alive and happy as I was in that moment. I took her in my arms and smothered her with kisses, undressing her as if I had never been with a woman before. Our lovemaking that night was the most intense it had ever been. We devoured every part of each other's bodies as if there was no tomorrow

– and who knows, maybe there wasn't.

The scent of her perfume and her sex, made even more powerful when aroused, kept me perpetually excited, and to hear her endearing Hungarian words of love was music to my ears. I could not possibly imagine such happiness ever again.

In the morning, I awoke after a deep and satisfying sleep with our arms and legs entwined. Ilona was still sleeping, her hair partially damp from a night of lovemaking. I gently tidied loose strands from her forehead and kissed her partially opened lips. 'Good morning, my darling.'

She opened her eyes and smiled. 'Oh, how I've dreamt of this. It kept me going,' she said, stretching her body.

'I too, although I admit there were times when I thought you might not come back.'

She lit up a cigarette while I went dragged myself from the bed to make us coffee. 'I'm going to spoil you,' I said, looking across the room at her naked body, with her well-shaped breasts and rosy pink nipples, the soft mound of golden pubic hair between her thighs inviting me to thrust myself between them again.

When the coffee was ready, I took it over on a small tray. With it was a small, prettily wrapped present. 'Here you are, my queen.'

Her smile radiated warmth in what had become a soulless apartment in her absence.

She untied the ribbon and carefully removed the paper, revealing a turquoise velvet box inscribed with the logo and name of the best jeweller in Istanbul in gold on the top. Her eyes widened. 'What's this? A brooch? A pair of earrings?'

I watched her face as she brought it closer, opened it slightly, and peeked inside. 'Édes kedvesem!' she exclaimed. 'A ring!' She took it out and stared at it for a few seconds. 'Emerald and diamonds: it's beautiful.' I took it from her and slipped it on her finger. She held her hand in the air, her fingers wide as she admired it. 'It must have cost a fortune.'

'I'm going to ask Dorothy for a divorce,' I said. 'I can't live without you – I love you that much.'

She put her hand down on the bed and her smile faded. 'Elliot!'

'Please tell me you'll marry me when this war is over.'

There was a flicker in her eyes, akin to a rabbit caught in headlights. She took the ring off and handed it to me.

'You shouldn't have bought it. It's bad luck.'

To say that I was shocked was an understatement. 'I love you, Ilona, more than I've ever loved anyone in my life. We can live wherever you want. If you want to go back to Hungary, I will go with you. I'll learn Hungarian, get a job, and look after you. You will not want for anything.' I realised I was sounding desperate.

'Stop! I told you it's bad luck. I also told you I wasn't the marrying kind when we met. Have you forgotten?'

'Ilona!' I had not envisioned this outcome and was overcome with frustration. 'What's bad luck? You sound like a gypsy talking gibberish, with their fortune-telling and curses.'

She sat up in bed and pulled the sheet over her, clenching it between her hands. 'Don't mock me. The war is not over.' She got up and started to dress.

I pulled her back down on the bed. 'I thought you loved me as I love you.'

She lowered her eyes. 'I want you to put this beautiful ring away. Maybe when the war is over, you can give it to me then. For the moment, let us savour what we have.'

I was exasperated. 'Are you listening? I love you and I want a divorce so that I can spend the rest of my life with you.'

She kissed me passionately. 'Now is not the time. Let us not forget why we are here.'

I was stunned. What I thought – that she loved me as I loved her – appeared to be wrong, but she assured me that was not so. She loved me and I must trust her.

I watched her tidy herself up as I had done so many times before and then she left.

'Will I see you later?' I asked, miserably.

'Of course, but not tonight. I have to see Sam.'

'Maybe the day after we could go to Büyükada and get a hotel. Spend the night out of the city as we have spoken about in the past. Before you start work at the club again.'

'I'd like that.'

After she left I sat there on the bed with its crumpled bed sheets, the apartment filled with her smell again, twirling the ring between my fingers. What a fool I'd been. She'd never once said she loved me.

We never did take that trip to Büyükada. OSS put a stop to it. Sam cautioned me, saying that things were at an all-time low with the Turks after the Cairo Conference and I must carry out surveillance work on the employees at Semperit Rubber. I asked him what was happening about the names mentioned in the secret messages, especially those who had come under Macfarland's wing. He said he was looking into them, in particular Alfred Schwarz, but that if Macfarland got wind of it, he would likely be sent back to Cairo.

Sam and I continued meeting at Mustafa's and exchanged news there. Neither Mustafa nor his wife mentioned Füsun and her family at all. We had more important things to discuss. The Turkish politicians were deliberately stalling for time. İnönü let the British know that without efficient weapons, they would never be able to stop a German attack coming from Greece and Bulgaria. Foreign Minister Menemencioğlu was particularly incensed about the British thinking they could send planes to Turkey right under the German's noses and not expect them to react. By the middle of February, Churchill felt the Allies were clutching at straws and their Turkish policy was turning into a failure. This was not helped by the fact that Roosevelt was not in favour of bringing Turkey into the war, but it was said that if Turkey continued with its unfavourable Allied policy, she would find herself alone after the war.

Sam made the comment that the Germans always seemed to be aware of any talks between the Allies and the Turks and that there must be a mole somewhere, but where? In a city full of spies, that was like looking for a needle in a haystack.

CHAPTER 12

ON MY FREE evenings, I went back to seeing Ilona perform with the band at the Rose Noir. Boris's sprits were high because she brought back the customers who had gone over to his competitors. I watched her every move, listened to every word of her songs, noting how she was able to rouse the audience as much as she did me. This time the band performed a few new songs – lively Hungarian romantic ones with more than a tinge of melancholy. By all accounts, Hungary was not in a good situation. By sending men to fight alongside the Germans, the Hungarian expeditionary force had suffered a crushing defeat at Voronezh in western Russia that cost it much of its manpower and equipment. Rumours had it that Hitler no longer trusted Prime Minister Miklós Kállay, who we knew had secretly approached the US in the event of an Axis defeat. So far they had managed to avoid sending all their Jews to the death camps, but there were still many others in the country whose life hung in the balance. Ilona didn't like to talk about this and I began to accept that is why she had refused my proposal.

Most evenings we spent together as we had always done. Occasionally we went out to dinner, but something felt wrong. It was as if we were living on borrowed time. It only made our lovemaking all the more intense. Then less than a month after she had been back, Sam told me they were sending her back to Hungary. I protested because of the tension there, but that meant nothing.

'Messner urgently needs a radio and more money. When this gets to him, we will be in a position to parachute our men in to liaise with the resistance on the ground. This is what we've been aiming for. We have to send her. It's even more vital now.'

Sadly, I understood. When we were alone, Ilona refused to talk about it. 'Just make love to me, édesem, like you always do. I want to remember these moments when I am away from you.'

The subject of the ring, divorce, marriage, was not brought up again. A few days before she left Istanbul, she had more meetings with OSS to which I was not privy, and although she always returned to me in a happy mood, I felt she was apprehensive. I only asked her once about her meetings and she scolded me like a naughty boy. Returning to the worsening situation in Budapest was a topic sure to dampen our love life, so I stopped talking about it. The night she left, she came to see me at the apartment to say goodbye. As before, Sam would not let me see her off at Sirkeci. She wore the same ruby-coloured suit and fox fur that she had worn the night she returned. On her head was a matching hat with a wide brim.

'Édes drágám, should anything happen to me, promise me that you will never forget me.'

I held her in my arms. Ilona was a strong woman but on this occasion she was trembling. I lifted her chin towards me. 'Never! Do you hear – never!' I saw the tears well up in her eyes and for once I had to be strong. 'Now come along or Sam will think you've changed your mind.' It was a feeble attempt to be light-hearted. 'I'll get you a taxi.'

I picked up her suitcase and we left the apartment. The weather was warmer, heralding a beautiful spring that I told her we'd enjoy together when she returned. I held the taxi door while she slipped into the back seat.

'Take care, Elliot.' She blew me a kiss.

I waved her goodbye, watching her wave back with a gloved hand through the back window. She looked so beautiful.

In the days after she left, I tried to occupy myself the best I could, but the nights were always the worst. I couldn't go to bed without imagining her next to me, whispering sweet words of endearment in Hungarian as we made love. After few weeks I was back to my normal duties with

OSS and reporting on the war for the newspapers. In the evenings, I often took long walks thinking about how life would be after the war. One evening Sam came round to see me. By the look on his face, I knew something terrible had happened. I braced myself for what he was about to say.

'Sit down, Elliot. I've got some rather bad news.'

'For God's sake, tell me. Is it Ilona?'

'Get us a drink, will you? It's worse than that. The Maier-Messner Network has been blown. It's finished – all over.'

I almost dropped the bottle of whisky. 'My God, Sam, it can't be possible. We've been so careful.'

Throughout the next few hours he told me everything he knew. Dulles had had a meeting with Messner and Issakides and they told him they were being watched. They also told him about our plans to deliver money and a radio to Budapest and expected the delivery soon. 'Something else,' Sam said. 'He was worried that we weren't acting quick enough in parachuting agents into Austria as he was sure the Soviets were already doing that.'

'But we talked about sending parachutists in?' I replied.

'I tried to initiate this earlier and was told to wait until it was safe and we could establish contact.'

'Why has Istanbul been so damned slow to act? It makes me ill to think about it. Everything that has gone higher up the chain has been ignored and now this.'

Sam continued. 'In the meantime, one of the main men in the network, Walter Caldonazzi, was picked up in Vienna and interrogated at the Gestapo headquarters in the Hotel Metropole. Another man was picked up a few days later, and the following week, two Gestapo agents seized the priest, Maier, at his church immediately after he had conducted mass and they took him to the Hotel Metropole.

'This is where it ends. Possibly a week later, we cannot say for sure, Messner and someone else, most likely his secretary, arrived in Budapest for their usual rendezvous where an intermediary would hand them the radio and the money. Messner was ambushed and taken back to

Gestapo Headquarters in Vienna. Dulles checked to be sure it wasn't just a rumour before we were told. We are waiting for more news.'

'And Ilona?' I could barely bring myself to say her name.

'Neither Dulles or Cairo has mentioned her. Let's take that as good news.' Over the course of the conversation, we drank half a bottle of whisky. 'Come on,' Sam said after a while. 'You're not staying here alone. We're going to Ilios's tonight. You can stay there for a few days, just in case anyone comes here and tries to bump you off. The Gestapo will be watching all of Messner's contacts now. We must lie low for a while.'

On the way to Ilios's, we made a detour to see what was going on at the offices of Semperit Rubber. As we'd expected, it was closed. Under the watchful eyes of the Turks, and careful not to make trouble, the Germans asked all the employees to report to them where they would undergo "questioning". It was highly likely they would be escorted back to Vienna.

Over the next few weeks we heard of more arrests in Austria. I was angry that OSS had sent Ilona back when they knew the situation was precarious, but what could I have done? I believed she understood the situation only too well, which was why I had sensed a subtle change in her.

In this fog of uncertainty, we discovered that Gustav Rudiger, the local representative at Semperit Istanbul and close friend of Messner, had Abwehr links, but it was not known if this was to maintain cordial relations with the Germans as there was no evidence against him. Sam and I trusted him completely as from the very beginning he had tried to forge an alliance between the CASSIA spy ring and the Allied powers together with Messner. Within Istanbul, he was the one privy to the industrial decision-making going on within the Reich. He was certainly committed to helping the CASSIA Network, but he was the one working with Alfred Schwarz, the name that cropped up in the secret messages, and who was still working for Macfarland. Schwarz had attempted to get Rudiger to go Budapest to find out what happened, but wisely, he refused. It was safer in Istanbul and so far he'd managed to evade the Germans. This move worried Sam and I, and we urged the powers that be to keep an eye on him and keep him safe.

The weeks passed and we heard nothing more. Throughout all this, I couldn't stop thinking about Ilona. I was at my wit's end wondering if she had been caught too, but no one seemed to be able to find out anything about her. We even tried checking if her band was playing anywhere, but they too seemed to have vanished. Not knowing was killing me.

After some consideration, I told Sam I wanted to be parachuted into Austria. That way I could find out what really took place. I not only wanted to know what had happened to the network, I wanted to find out what happened to Ilona too, but I was told by Sam that she hadn't gone to Austria. Budapest was her destination and it was impossible for me to get there.

'A bad idea,' Sam said. 'A noble one, but foolish. Besides, we can still use you here.'

In the meantime, things in Turkey were turning in our favour. In April, the government halted its sales of chromite to Germany and Foreign Minister Menemencioğlu resigned, due in part to a confrontation between the UK and Turkey about German ships going through the Turkish Straits. The Allies landed in Normandy in early June and were making their way towards Paris. Finally, the Turks finally broke off relations with Germany in August.

With the network disbanded, I had the choice to continue with OSS or go back to SOE. In the end the decision was made for me. Jack Mackintosh asked to see me and offered me a mission in Greece. I had never been to Greece, but he knew I spoke Greek.

'There has been another massacre,' he said, 'this time in the village of Distomo in Boeotia on 10 June. Units of the Waffen-SS *Polizei* Division looted and burned the village, resulting in the deaths of 218 civilians. There have been many more massacres – I am sure you are aware of that. Come back to us and help the resistance. We need your expertise and it's better than sitting around here doing nothing.'

'I'm not sitting around doing nothing.' The way I replied told him that I was frustrated and I apologised.

'Since when has it been safe to be parachuted into enemy territory? Greece is not safe either.'

'You are right, but at least in Greece we have men on the ground–and a strong resistance. You cannot say that about Austria. If they catch you, you will be shot on sight.'

The decision was made for me. I thought I would go mad if I didn't stop thinking about Ilona. I needed something to take my mind off her. And then there was Leila and Stavros. I wanted to avenge their deaths.

I spent one last evening with Sam at the Park Hotel and told him of my decision.

'I aim to go to Vienna when it's safe,' he said. 'Maybe I will meet you there. In the meantime, if I hear anything about Ilona, I will let you know – wherever you are. Good luck.'

There was one thing I needed to do before I left Istanbul. I headed to the Galata Bridge with the ring that I'd bought for Ilona. I looked at it one more time before lifting my arm to throw it into the water. I was a split second from doing it when I noticed an elderly couple fishing nearby. They were just like many others who fished there, all hoping to get something to feed themselves: families who scratched a living the best way they could when there was little work. I walked over and tapped the man on the shoulder.

'Here,' I said. 'I no longer have need for this. Please accept it for your wife.'

The couple opened the box as I walked away and stared at the ring in disbelief. At least I had made someone happy rather than throw it away.

I left Turkey for SOE's headquarters in Cairo and was briefed for my new mission. I was dropped into Greece two weeks later and made my way north to Epirus to help EDES, the National Republic Greek League, to work with Napoleon Zervas, a former army officer and republican. Throughout the occupation, Zervas ran a strong guerrilla force working with his rivals in Epirus, a particularly poor mountainous region, and most of the support he received had been provided by the British. It didn't take me long to realise that although the Greek resistance had fought bravely against the Italians and Germans, the various ideological factions were now in the process of setting themselves up against each other for when the Germans left, and I feared for the future of Greece.

One thing did hearten me though. Turkey eventually decided to break off diplomatic ties with Germany and join the Allies. On 2 August 1944, İnönü and his government severed diplomatic relations with Germany, forcing von Papen to return to Berlin.

On 23 August 1944, at a meeting at his headquarters, Adolf Hitler told Field Marshal Maximilian von Weichs, the commander of the German forces in the Balkans, that because the Romanian oil fields were lost as the Soviets had taken Romania, and the resistance was inflicting serious casualties in Greece, it would be wise to begin preparations for a withdrawal at once.

German troops evacuated Athens on 12 October 1944. Most left Greece and Albania via Yugoslavia and, along with other members of SOE, I followed them. A month earlier, in September 1944, the Allies had launched major offensives there, aiming to frustrate their movements through Serbia, Croatia, and Slovenia, and the British sent a powerful combat unit composed of artillery and engineers, which Tito's Partisans were desperately in need of. Due to the combined spirit of resistance and badly needed British artillery, the Partisans now controlled the entire eastern half of Yugoslavia – Serbia, Macedonia, and Montenegro – as well as most of the Dalmatian coast.

From Yugoslavia, I made my way to Austria, eventually joining the American troops who crossed the Austrian border on 26 April 1945, followed by French troops on 29 April and the British on 8 May. Soviet troops had already crossed the former Austrian border in Burgenland, Lower Austria, in March and were already dismantling Nazi signs and wreaking havoc throughout the country. The Red Army lost 17,000 lives alone in the Battle of Vienna and ultimately the Soviets assumed control over Austrian oil what would become their zone.

Up until the end of July 1945 we'd had no first-hand intelligence from Eastern Austria and arriving there was a great shock. Everywhere was devastation. So many burnt out villages and roadside graves that it was a nightmare I would never forget. I ended up in Vienna when the first Americans arrived there at the end of July 1945. The beautiful city lay in ruins. There I met up with Sam at the prestigious Sacher's Hotel next to the opera, which had also been bombed. Together we tried to find out what had happened to the CASSIA Network – in particular, Messner and the priest, Maier. The news was shocking. Barbara Issakides was one of the few to survive and she came to see us. We barely recognised her, she was so gaunt. Apparently she survived because she had stomach problems and was kept in hospital for months. We assumed that this was a combination of a sympathetic doctor and her international fame as a pianist.

On 9 July 1945, the Allies agreed on the borders of their occupation zones. The French and American zones bordered those countries' zones near France and Germany, and the Soviet zone bordered future Warsaw Pact states. East Tyrol, Carinthia, and Styria were assigned to the British Zone.

The Gestapo had tried to set members of the group against each other whilst they were in the Liesl Prison and under torture, but the group realised what was going on. In October 1944, a show trial took place at the Vienna Regional Court and after two days, sentences were passed on ten of the members. They were sent to Mauthausen Concentration Camp. Walter Caldonazzi was beheaded at the Vienna Regional Court in January 1945. Maier was brought back to Vienna and beheaded on the evening of March 22, and Messner was gassed at Mauthausen just before the camp was liberated. It was hard for us to digest this information. The network had done so much for the Allies.

In a gesture of thanks, Issakides gave a piano concert in Vienna for the Allies, and OSS reciprocated by sponsoring a fine reception in her honour. Sam and I were there, applauding both her skill and her bravery.

'Well, Elliot, what are you going to do now?' he asked. 'I am going to Nuremberg, where there is to be an International Military Tribunal for those responsible for what's happened – Hermann Göring, Himmler, Ribbentrop, and many more.'

'I might join you,' I said. 'I still want to find out what happened to Ilona.'

I will never forget the way Sam looked at me. 'Elliot, forget her. We think she probably evaded capture.'

'Then all the more reason for me to find her.'

'The Soviets occupy Hungary at the moment. It's not wise.'

'I don't care.'

'Elliot, listen to me. You would be going on a wild goose chase.'

'Why's that?'

'Because...' He faltered before finishing the sentence. 'Because Ilona is not her real name. It was the one Macfarland gave her. Just as you are not Elliot.'

I was so shocked I couldn't speak. I was so taken in by the woman I loved that such an obvious thing as that had never occurred to me.

'And I suppose you won't tell me her real name, will you?' I said after a while.

Sam shook his head. 'Even if I knew – and I don't – I wouldn't tell you.' He put his hand on my shoulder. 'Go home, old chap. Your work is finished here.' I looked at him with tears in my eyes. 'One day we will have a beer together – in England – and I promise you, if I do find out what happened to her, I will let you know.'

CHAPTER 13

DOROTHY WAS AT the station to greet me and welcomed me with open arms and sweet words. Everything was just as it was when I left. The garden was immaculate, the view across the green fields was bucolic and serene, and most of all Dorothy was the same loving and attentive person I'd left. She hadn't changed at all, but it wasn't easy to adjust to life back in England. I was no longer Elliot, I was George again. That took some getting used to.

Reading the newspapers about the Nuremberg Trials, the crimes against humanity, and the concentration camps, I began to sink into depression. I'd longed for the war to be over and now it was, I felt lost, that I hadn't done enough. I couldn't stop thinking about the fate of Father Maier and Messner, the silver-haired gentleman I'd come to know, albeit at a distance, and others like them. I was told that was normal, that there were mental scars that would take time to heal. It was easy for others to dish out well-meaning advice. They hadn't lived life on the edge. After a few months, the distance between Dorothy and me grew wider. She kept asking what was wrong and wished I would talk to her more.

'Dorothy,' I said one day, after she'd questioned if I still loved her, 'I'm sorry I seem so distant. It's not you, it's me. During the war I belonged to another world. That world won us our freedom, but it came at a cost and there are things I saw and did that I would rather forget. Many brave souls perished. I beg of you, if we are to live together in peace

– and right now, peace is what I crave – don't keep asking me questions because I cannot and will not answer you.'

She gave a bitter laugh. 'The Official Secrets Act, I suppose.'

I looked her straight in the face. Her eyes had lost their sparkle and I felt responsible. 'That's right.'

She reached for my hand. 'It's alright, my darling. Life must go on and so I will be patient until the time comes when you are able to put it behind you.'

She snuggled in my arms and a tear slipped down my cheek, which she gently wiped away with her finger. A sad silence settled between us. I couldn't tell her about my life in Istanbul, what I'd seen in Greece, or about the horrors of Mauthausen, and I certainly couldn't tell her about Ilona. It would crush her spirit. I wished with all my heart I could say those words she wanted to hear – I love you – three little words I'd said so often to Ilona, but the words stuck in my throat. How I'd longed for Ilona to say those words too. Now love seemed elusive. I didn't even know what the word meant any more.

'I know it must be hard to come back after all you've been through,' she said in her soft, caring voice. 'It can't have been a bed of roses, but you'll soon be back to normal, you'll see.' She gave a little smile. 'You're a very brave man and I'm proud of you.'

A bed of roses! Dorothy was a smart woman, but she had no idea. In her innocence, she was trying to make me feel better, and that only made me feel worse. I continued to hold her but all I could hear was a sultry voice from the past – *Édes drágám! Should anything happen to me, promise me that you won't forget me?* How could I? All the Ilonas, Leilas, Messners, Issakides, Maiers, and others like them. *They* were the brave ones.

Sitting in our cosy cottage with its chintz armchairs and sideboards filled with meaningless ornaments and photographs from another time, none of it seemed real. It was as if I'd been an actor in a play and the curtains had closed, the audience had cheered and left, and all that was left of me – or the shell of me – was a person standing on an empty stage as the lights dimmed. It was all over. I felt numb.

A few months later, the telephone rang and Dorothy answered it.

'Yes, just a moment, I'll get him for you.' She covered the receiver with her hand. 'It's for you. He says his name is Sam Johnson.'

I took the receiver from her. 'Sam! This is a surprise. It's been a while now.'

Sam said he was in the area for a day or two and asked if I'd like to meet him at the Hare and Hounds later that evening. He wanted to have a little chat. Guessing that this had something to do with my war past, Dorothy said she would stay at home, which relieved me greatly as I thought he might have news of Ilona. I couldn't think of any other reason he would contact me.

Out of sheer nervousness and anticipation at what he wanted to say, I was there fifteen minutes before the appointed time and found a place next to the fireplace. I was on my second pint when I saw him pull up in the carpark in a smart black Wolseley. He opened the boot to retrieve a large carrier bag and strode across the gravel in his usual confident manner, ducking slightly when he entered the old pub with its low-beamed ceilings.

'Good to see you, George. You look well. The English countryside does wonders for you.'

'How are you, Sam? What brings you all this way?' I ordered him a pint while he settled himself into one of the leather armchairs.

'I do enjoy these places,' he said. 'Rather quaint, and the beer is good too.'

I came straight to the point. 'Have you brought news of Ilona?'

He sipped on his beer and then shook his head. 'Sorry, old man. Nothing on that front, I'm afraid. We've given up looking now – too many other things to contend with.' He sat back in the chair and gave a deep sigh. 'You know, you really must let go of the past.'

'Then what brings you here? I'm sure it can't be because you miss my company.'

He looked around the half-empty pub to make sure we weren't being overheard. 'I'm working for MI6 now. They want someone who can liaise with the Americans so we're recruiting. I'm looking for the best talent: people with proven credentials and proficient in languages.

I heard that SOE has been disbanded and that you are without a job and I thought of you. Are you willing to come back into the fold? You will be well looked after.'

'What's the assignment?'

'Top secret as you can imagine, but I can give you a hint. As you know, we are now in another war of sorts. We have entered a new phase, one where there is geopolitical tension between the United States, the Soviet Union, and our allies. Our mission now is to keep a lid on Communists, authoritarian states, and right-wing dictatorships. There are uprisings across the world and who knows where it will end? I believe the writer George Orwell calls it a "cold war".'

'So are you intending to send me to Berlin?'

'We would like you in infiltrate into the Russian sector – under another identity, of course.'

'I don't speak Russian.'

'With your aptitude for languages, you could learn it in no time. We'd be sending you on a six month training course first.'

'What would my role be?'

'To pick up secrets and work with our other agents there.' He ordered another beer for us both before continuing. 'We also want to infiltrate the Hungarian Secret Service too.'

'I don't speak Hungarian either.'

Sam sighed again. 'You might even find out what happened to Ilona.' He saw the flicker in my eye. 'Think about it.'

At the mention of Ilona, the old bitterness surfaced. 'Finding the illusive Ilona was *your* business, Sam. OSS had responsibility for the CASSIA Network, and you blew it through ineptitude. You failed to recognise the signs even though they stared you in the face.' After everything we'd gone through, it surprised me that I felt so cool towards him. Where once we had been friends, I no longer felt that close bond. Maybe it was because I was trying to put it all behind me. 'I won't put my life on the line again.'

Sam looked offended. 'Not even for God and country? Besides, Macfarland is not involved this time. It's MI6 not OSS.'

'They're all the same – all as bad as each other.'

Sam finished his beer and stood up. 'Well, George, I'll give you a day or two to think about it. If the answer is yes, you can reach me at this number.' He put his card on the table. 'And remember, this time the money is good. It will set you up for life.' He handed me the bag. 'By the way, these are for you. I picked them up in London.' I took a quick look inside. They were Greek records – Sofia Vembo, who had kept the home fires burning in Greece with her poignant music. I'd always considered her to be Greece's answer to Vera Lynn. 'I always realised what Greece meant to you and you hid it so well. Maybe this will remind you of her.'

With a civil war raging there as we spoke, I didn't need reminding.

We shook hands and he left. I sat back in the chair and watched him drive away, mulling over our conversation. I ordered another beer and picked up his card. Once upon a time, I would have jumped at such an opportunity, but the war had turned my life upside down and I no longer wanted to live on a razor's edge. In fact, I wanted nothing more to do with them. I tore the card up and threw it into the embers of the fire, watching the pieces curl into fine black slivers. Then I made my way back home.

I walked back to the cottage via a winding pathway, redolent with the scent of wildflowers in the evening breeze. For the first time since I'd returned, I noticed how beautiful and peaceful it was. When I returned to the cottage, Dorothy was in the kitchen putting the finishing touches to a pie and singing along to the Vera Lynn song "You'll Never Know" on the radio. I stood unseen in the doorway and listened to her for a moment or two as she sang the familiar refrain about the lover who will never know how much she cares.

"You went away and my heart went with you
I speak your name in my every prayer
If there is some other way to prove that I love you..."

I suddenly burst out laughing, which almost made her drop the pie. She looked bewildered. 'George! You gave me the fright of my life. What are you laughing at?'

I didn't know and I didn't care. I walked over to her, picked her up in my arms, and swirled her around the kitchen.

'Are you drunk?' she laughed.

'No, my darling, I'm not drunk, I'm just happy to be home.'

POSTSCRIPT

Midnight in Istanbul is a story centred on the WWII Austrian resistance group known by several names – 05, the Maier-Messner-Caldonazzi Network. OSS referred to them as CASSIA or the Maier-Messner group. In 1943 the internationally known Viennese pianist Barbara Issakides and Franz Josef Messner, the successful general director of Semperit, a major tyre manufacturer based in Vienna, openly discussed their plans and goals about the group with Allen Dulles, head of the OSS office in Bern, Switzerland. From then on, the resistance group was in continuous, albeit irregular, contact with them.

I first came across this group while researching a previous novel, *The Viennese Dressmaker*, but in that story, I used the information differently. The priest was based on Heinrich Maier and the baroness on Barbara Issakides. I was aware at the time that the Semperit office in Istanbul was a major factor in bringing down the group, and decided to leave that story for another time. As is often the case, going down the rabbit warren of research leads us to places we could never have imagined.

There were many Austrians opposed to the rise of Fascism and the Anschluss under Hitler, and most paid dearly with their lives for their opposition. Prior to the Anschluss, those deemed "trouble-makers" were being watched, and for the most part, this meant the outspoken Communists. Thousands were rounded up and imprisoned, but there were others who blended into mainstream society in a more discreet way.

Heinrich Maier (16 February 1908 – 22 March 1945) was one

of them. He was an Austrian Roman Catholic priest, and generally thought to be the founder of the Maier-Messner group. When the Nazis abolished religious instruction, Maier lost his job as a religion teacher in 1938, but remained chaplain in the parish of Gersthof-St. Leopold in Währing, Vienna. It was there, in 1940, that his political convictions against the Reich began and he set about contacting other like-minded groups. In the end he formed his own group together with the Tyrolean Catholic-monarchist resistance fighter, Walter Caldonazzi, from South Tyrol, and Franz Josef Messner (8 December 1896 – 23 April 1945) the Tyrolean director of the international Semperit Works. They advocated the following principle: "Every bomb that falls on armaments factories shortens the war and spares the civilian population."

The group he led was considered to be one of the most important for the Allies during World War II because it collected and passed on information about the locations, employees, and production of Nazi armaments factories. This information for targeted bombing by the Allies was passed on to middlemen in Switzerland to the British and Americans. At first, MI6 were dubious as it was hard to know what was going on in Austria, or Ostmark, as it became known after the Anschluss, which led to the group working with OSS.

On 27 April 1944, Maier stated that the group's strategy was to prevent further air strikes on Austrian cities and the civilian population; therefore, they would provide information about armaments factories. Together with Dr. Messner, they revealed important armament centres in Austria and elsewhere in the Reich. Via Walter Caldonazzi, the group also had contacts with Italian resistance groups through Italian construction workers.

One of the most important pieces of information concerned the V-2 rocket, which was produced by prisoners in concentration camps. The exact drawings of the V-2 rocket, the production of the Tiger Tank and Messerschmitt Bf109 and other weapons, were passed on via Maier's close relationship with the Vienna city commander, Heinrich "Rico" Stümpfl, a former officer of the Austro-Hungarian Army and Austrian Army who was ready to help them at all times. Precise location sketches and production figures for steel mills, weapons, ball bearings, the German production situation for synthetic rubber (Buna), and aircraft factories soon reached Allied general staffs. Maier's saying, based on Shakespeare's *Richard III*, "A kingdom for a ball bearing", was taken seriously by OSS.

Walter Caldonazzi used his contacts in the Heinkel factories in the Tyrol, where components for the Messerschmitt Me 163 Komet and V-2 rockets were manufactured. Information about the aircraft factory in Wiener Neustadt near Vienna, was also extremely important as it was the most important and largest German factory for the production of fighter aircraft at the time. Because of the information passed on, American and British bombers were able to strike armaments factories such as the secret V-rocket factory V-1 and V-2 at Peenemünde, and the Messerschmitt plants near Vienna.

These contributions by the group were crucial for Operation Crossbow and Operation Hydra, both preliminary missions for Operation Overlord. All of this information cannot be underestimated. It had the effect of shortening the war.

Messner also provided the first information about the mass murder of Jews from his Semperit plant near Auschwitz – the enormity of which amazed the Americans in Zurich and helped to sway OSS into helping them. In 1943, the British were still not convinced of the reliability of one of the Istanbul contact persons, Franz Josef Rüdiger, a Messner employee, and did not cooperate due to security concerns. After the arrests in 1944, there was little evidence to suggest Rudiger was a traitor, although he had links to the Abwehr, but that was viewed by Messner as normal to keep them on side.

When the arrests finally took place, some members of the group were arrested in February 1944 after being betrayed. Others were arrested later. Heinrich Maier was arrested on 28 March 1944 by the Gestapo in the sacristy after the holy mass and taken to the prison in the Gestapo Headquarters in the former Hotel Metropole on Morzinplatz. During the interrogations, Maier managed to both conceal the actions of the group and to exonerate other members. The Gestapo was unable to uncover the great importance of the resistance group.

Messner was arrested in Budapest in March when he was ambushed picking up a radio and money sent by OSS. Barbara Issakides was also arrested at this time.

The secret people's trials at the Vienna Regional Court were notorious. In the trial on 27 and 28 October 1944, a total of eight death sentences were imposed on Heinrich Maier, Walter Caldonazzi, Franz Josef Messner, Andreas Hofer, Josef Wyhnal, Hermann Klepell, Wilhelm Ritsch, and Clemens von Pausinger. The indictment was "preparation for treason". After the conviction, Maier was transferred to the Mauthausen concentration camp on 22 November 1944. He was severely tortured for months before his execution in the hope that he would reveal more information about the group. The concentration camp guards tied Maier to the window cross of a barracks without clothes and beat him mercilessly, but he said nothing.

Caldonazzi was beheaded at the Vienna Regional Court in January 1945 and Messner was executed at Mauthausen on 23 April 1945 at 1500 hours along with another thirty-nine prisoners. A senior squad leader reported, "The commander himself initiated the flow of poison gas." Twelve days after Messner's death, the US 11th Armored Division liberated Mauthausen. By then the Soviets had captured Vienna and the Hotel Metropole had been reduced to bombed-out ruins.

On 18 March 1945, Maier was brought back to Vienna together with three others. Heinrich Maier was beheaded in the Vienna Regional Court on 22 March 1945 at 6:40 p.m. Witnesses state that he approached death with a deeply impressive composure. His last words were "Long live Christ, the king! Long live Austria!" He was the last victim to be executed in Vienna in this manner before the liberation.

Barbara Issakides survived by being kept in the hospital due to stomach problems, but it is highly likely she was saved due to her notoriety as an international pianist and kindly doctors. As a thank you for their help, she did indeed play for OSS in Vienna. It was the last time she played in public.

But what of the others who were thought to have betrayed the group? Messner had his legitimate Semperit offices in Istanbul, as he did in many parts of the Reich, and also in Brazil, so his business naturally attracted engineers from the industrial, agricultural, and maritime sphere, but as has been stated, Istanbul was a nest of spies. All the secret agencies worked there and some were more thorough than others. There were spies and double agents, but much of the blame for lax security lies with OSS Istanbul itself. Unlike Harold Gibson of MI6, who was an experienced operator, the chief of OSS in Istanbul, Lanning Macfarland, hired the smooth-talking, shadowy Czech businessman, thirty-nine-year-old Alfred Schwarz, through Rüdiger, who was aware he worked for the Netherlands-based Philips & Company, the largest manufacturer of radios and radio tubes. Schwarz was given the code name DOGWOOD and it was he who brought in other dubious operators. All the agents had names of plants. As a primary agent, he recruited secondary agents and thorough checks were not made on some of them. Laufer, Hatz, and Kovess, were three such agents.

Laufer and Hatz were arrested in Budapest whilst giving money and a radio to the resistance but released soon after, something that always aroused suspicion. Hatz then reappeared back in Istanbul and was warned of his duplicity by William Donovan himself. He pointed the finger at Laufer, as did one of those captured at the time.

As for Turkey during World War II, the British always felt that Foreign Minister Menemencioğlu was pro-German. After his dismissal in 1944, the Turks moved in favour of the British and halted its sales of chromite to Germany. They broke off relations with Germany in August and declared war on the Axis powers in February 1945.

Much of the information gathered by the Allies at the various conferences was passed on to von Papen by the infamous spy Cicero.

The OSS was dissolved a month after the end of the war and intelligence tasks resumed by its successors, the Department of State's Bureau of Intelligence and Research (INR), and Allen Dulles became the first civilian director of the CIA during the early Cold War.

Apart from those names and organisations in the public domain, the storyline and main characters – Sam, Elliot, Ilona, Mustafa, and

Leila – are fictional, created to add drama to the novel. Secret messages using invisible ink, working with couriers and a handler, and a thorough knowledge of weapons in general, are all part of the tradecraft of a secret agent.

Last but not least, I would like to thank my good friend, author Sebnem E. Sanders, for helping me with the Turkish place names, words, and idioms. As with my other novel set in Turkey, *The Carpet Weaver of Uşak*, her knowledge of Turkey and the language has been invaluable.

ALSO BY THE AUTHOR

In the Shadow of the Pyrenees

The Song of the Partisans

The Viennese Dressmaker

The Secret of the Grand Hôtel du Lac

The Poseidon Network

Conspiracy of Lies

The Blue Dolphin

Code Name Camille (Novella)

The Embroiderer

The Carpet Weaver of Uşak

Seraphina's Song

Colours of Aegean Dreams: A Greek Odyssey
– A Colouring Book for Adults

Website:

www.kathryngauci.com

To sign up to my newsletter,
please visit my website and fill out the form.

AUTHOR BIOGRAPHY

Kathryn Gauci is a critically acclaimed international, bestselling, author who produces strong, colourful, characters and riveting storylines. She is the recipient of numerous major international awards for her works of historical fiction.

Kathryn was born in Leicestershire, England, and studied textile design at Loughborough College of Art and later at Kidderminster College of Art and Design where she specialised in carpet design and technology. After graduating, she spent a year in Vienna, Austria, before moving to Greece to work as carpet designer in Athens for six years. There followed another brief period in New Zealand before eventually settling in Melbourne, Australia.

Before turning to writing full-time, Kathryn ran her own textile design studio in Melbourne for over fifteen years, work which she enjoyed tremendously as it allowed her the luxury of travelling worldwide, often taking her off the beaten track and exploring other cultures. *The Embroiderer* is her first novel; a culmination of those wonderful years of design and travel, and especially of those glorious years in her youth living and working in Greece. It has since been followed by more novels set in both Greece and Turkey. *Seraphina's Song*, *The Carpet Weaver of Uşak*, *The Poseidon Network*, and *The Blue Dolphin: A WWII Novel*.

Code Name Camille, written as part of *The Darkest Hour Anthology: WWII Tales of Resistance*, became a *USA TODAY* Bestseller in the first week of publication.

The Secret of the Grand Hôtel du Lac became an Amazon Best Seller in both German Literature and French Literature.

Both *The Secret of the Grand Hôtel du Lac* and *The Blue Dolphin* **received** The Hemingway Finalist Award 2021.

The Poseidon Network received The Hemingway Award 2020 – 1st Place Best in Category – Chanticleer International Book Awards (CIBA) 20th Century Wartime Fiction.

The Viennese Dressmaker received The Hemingway Award 2022 – 1st Place Best in Category – Chanticleer International Book Awards (CIBA) 20th Century Wartime Fiction and The Coffee Pot Book Club Book of the Year Award – Gold Medal 2022 – 20th Century Historical Fiction

In the Shadow of the Pyrenees received The Hemingway Award 2023 – 1st Place Best in Category – Chanticleer International Book Awards (CIBA) 20th Century Wartime Fiction and The Coffee Pot Book Club Book of the Year Award – Gold Medal 2023 – 20th Century Historical Fiction

The Song of the Partisans received the Readers' Favourite 2023 Gold Medal Award for Military Fiction.

Milton Keynes UK
Ingram Content Group UK Ltd.
UKHW020637200524
442968UK00001B/181